IMAGES OF WAR

THE SOVIET-AFGHAN WAR

A considerable proportion of the Soviet tank force consisted of the aging T-55 main battle tank. Around 50,000 T-54/55 tanks were built between 1954 and 1981. Many were issued to the Soviet motor rifle divisions and would bear the brunt of the fighting in Afghanistan. This particular example belongs to the Polish Army. (*Graham Thompson*)

IMAGES OF WAR

THE SOVIET-AFGHAN WAR

RARE PHOTOGRAPHS FROM WARTIME ARCHIVES

ANTHONY TUCKER-JONES

Pen & Sword
MILITARY

First published in Great Britain in 2012 by
PEN & SWORD MILITARY
an imprint of
Pen & Sword Books Ltd,
47 Church Street,
Barnsley,
South Yorkshire
S70 2AS

A CIP record for this book is available from the British Library.

ISBN 978 184884 578 7

Typeset by Chic Media Ltd

Printed and bound by CPI Group (UK) Ltd, Croydon, CR0 4YY

Pen & Sword Books Ltd incorporates the Imprints of
Pen & Sword Aviation, Pen & Sword Family History, Pen & Sword
Maritime, Pen & Sword Military, Pen & Sword Discovery, Wharncliffe
Local History, Wharncliffe True Crime, Wharncliffe Transport, Pen &
Sword Select, Pen & Sword Military Classics, Leo Cooper,
The Praetorian Press, Remember When, Seaforth Publishing and
Frontline Publishing.

For a complete list of Pen & Sword titles please contact
Pen & Sword Books Limited
47 Church Street, Barnsley, South Yorkshire, S70 2AS, England
E-mail: enquiries@pen-and-sword.co.uk
Website: www.pen-and-sword.co.uk

Contents

Introduction

The Soviet–Afghan War was a particularly brutal conflict pitting political dogma against religious ideology – namely Communism versus Islam. It was also an uneven struggle, with a modern, highly mobile and very well-equipped army seeking to crush lightly and ill-armed guerrillas. The Soviet Union threw its tanks, jet fighters and attack helicopters not only at the resistance, but also at the Afghan population. This was designed to deny the Mujahideen or 'God's Warriors' a safe haven from which to operate and in the process caught civilians in the brutal crossfire.

The guerrilla war fought against Moscow's intervention in Afghanistan during 1979–89 has been described as the largest national rising of the twentieth century. It has also been compared with the Yugoslav partisan war fought during the Second World War against the Nazis. What is so remarkable is that civilians, largely equipped with just light weapons, successfully resisted the mighty Soviet armed forces for over nine long years, ironically echoing subsequent Taliban efforts against Britain and America.

A year longer than that other protracted conflict during the 1980s the Iran–Iraq War, the Afghanistan struggle saw constant widespread guerrilla and conventional warfare, ranging from hit-and-run ambushes to large-scale divisional/corps-level offensive sweeps. It also saw the intervention of a former Superpower fail, where Britain had also once failed. Ultimately, despite its military muscle, the Soviet Union proved unable or unwilling to defeat the warlike Afghan tribesmen.

My involvement in the Soviet–Afghan War was initially as a young analyst recruited by British Defence Intelligence to work as the Soviet Warsaw Pact politico-economic desk officer. This role functioned alongside the Afghan cell that was tasked with monitoring the progress of the fighting.

One of the primary prerequisites for waging successful guerrilla warfare is having a secure base from which to operate. The Mujahideen were lucky in that both Iran and Pakistan turned a blind eye to their activities, as well as allowing them to smuggle arms over the borders. Additionally, Afghanistan ended up with the largest refugee population in the world, allowing, as Mao Tse-Tung put it, the guerrillas to swim like fish in the sea of the people.

Intelligence reports showed that no matter how many resources and firepower Moscow poured into Afghanistan the country proved to be a bottomless pit. The Mujahideen with their apparent disregard for life proved to be plucky and determined adversaries. They made it clear they would not stop fighting until the Soviet Union withdrew. Russian General Boris Gromov later described the Soviet–Afghan War as 'an irreparable political mistake by the Soviet leadership'. This salutary lesson was to be ignored by Washington and its allies in 2001.

British and American interest in the war peaked following the provision of US Stinger surface-to-air missiles (SAMs) to the Mujahideen in the late 1980s as the culmination of the CIA's massive Operation Cyclone. The operation, which ran for seven years, was one of the most costly and longest CIA missions ever undertaken. It provided the resistance with funding, weapons and training. Once the American SAMs had been delivered, everyone was waiting for the demise of Soviet airpower – especially their powerful attack helicopters.

For a long time, though, the Mujahideen had no real effective answer to the death-dealing Hind Mi-24 gunships. Mujahideen attacks and ambushes were regularly responded to by these helicopters with their devastating array of chain gun, missiles, rockets and bombs. Robust and well armoured, the Hind proved very difficult to shoot down. The Stinger helped change all that.

By the late 1980s the West became particularly obsessed with Moscow's constant delays with its much-publicised withdrawal from Afghanistan. No one could really believe that after a decade the Soviet armed forces were really calling it a day.

The Soviet participation in Operation Magistral in the winter of 1987 posed a dilemma for Moscow, as it was trying to extricate itself from the Afghanistan imbroglio. By mounting such a large-scale operation, Moscow appeared to be escalating the war despite its genuine withdrawal overtures. Nevertheless, the fall of Khost to the Mujahideen would have been a military and psychological blow to the already demoralised Afghan Army, which in turn would have increased its reliance on the Soviet 40th Army. Furthermore, the Soviets feared a rival Mujahideen government in Khost could present a viable political rallying point just as they were about to pull out. Moscow needed to save face.

The war in Afghanistan was televised 'live' for the first time in the Soviet Union on 19 December 1987, with a report on the offensive. There was no mention of Soviet involvement in the battle. The decision to show the fighting at Khost was part of a move by Moscow to prepare the Soviet public for the withdrawal and to show the Afghan Army bearing the brunt of the war. However, the Afghan troops fought for almost four weeks and progress was painfully slow. With the Afghan Army having made little headway, the Soviets were forced to commit their paratroops – on the very same day as the television broadcast – to what should have been solely an Afghan Army operation.

At the time of the withdrawal in early 1989 Moscow was understandably tight lipped about the economic and human cost of the conflict. The truth was that it had bled dry the Soviet defence budget and undermined the standing of the Soviet Army. 'When I was asked what the most difficult task was during the pullout, and what the main outcome was, I say believe me – that we emerged with minimum losses,' said Soviet 40th Army commander General Boris Gromov.

This book is intended to provide a visual record of the Soviet–Afghan conflict, so the accompanying text can only touch upon the key aspects of the fighting. Anyone seeking a fuller account may like to consult my *The Rise of Militant Islam* (also published by Pen & Sword), which covers the numerous wars in Afghanistan and their ramifications in much greater depth.

Photograph Sources

The author is grateful for the assistance of his contacts in Afghanistan past and present. Many of the images in this book originally came via the Afghanistan Information Office (AIO), the Afghanistan Support Committee (ASC) and the Islamic Alliance of Afghan Mujahideen (IAAM), who sought to publicise the guerrillas' cause throughout the 1980s. In addition photographs have been drawn from a number of private collections, including the author's, and many of them have never been published before.

In particular the author is very indebted to Igor Bondarets, Erwin Franzen and Julian Gearing for making their collections available for this project. Both Erwin and Julian were print journalists who covered the war from the perspective of the resistance and travelled into Afghanistan on numerous occasions, risking life and limb. On the other side of the conflict Igor specialised in the Soviet armed forces deployed to Afghanistan. Images have also been drawn from unclassified US Department of Defense holdings, which in turn were taken from a variety of Mujahideen sources seeking to highlight Soviet aggression against the Afghan people.

The author is responsible for the final selection of photographs and he hopes that they go some way to illustrate the varied aspects of the conflict. Many of the original negatives, especially in the case of Erwin Franzen's photos, are unfortunately in bad shape, and although digitisation has helped tidy them up, a few remain blurred or grainy. Nevertheless, while the quality of some may vary, the composition and content provides a insight into the daily prosecution of the now largely forgotten Soviet–Afghan War.

Readers may also be interested in the author's companion volume *Images of War: Kalashnikov in Combat*, which charts the use of the AK-47 in the various conflicts fought in Afghanistan.

Chapter One

Cold War Stand Off

Now a decade old, Operation Enduring Freedom, designed to oust the Taliban from power, is an echo of a much bloodier war that was fought in Afghanistan over thirty years ago. Those who recall how grim Kabul was in the late 1970s will know that it became even grimmer after the arrival of Soviet tanks, jets and helicopters. Once more, geography, as in the earlier Korean and Vietnam wars, was to preclude the effective use of armour in Afghanistan. It was as if the Russians never bothered to heed any of the lessons of these previous conflicts and proceeded to learn the hard way – from scratch.

The Soviet Union was at the height of its military power by the late 1970s. It was a vast monolith whose military resources were only rivalled by the world's other Superpower – the United States of America. Every year during Moscow's Red Square military parades the Soviet armed forces put on displays of equipment bristling with firepower, designed to impress the population and cow its enemies. These parades also served to tip off Western intelligence of the existence of new equipment. The Soviets could not resist showing off.

For the previous two decades the Warsaw Pact and NATO had been at military loggerheads, facing off against each other in armed confrontation across central Europe in what was known as the Cold War. It was largely the threat of mutually assured destruction, should conflict break out and escalate to a nuclear war, that kept the two sides from coming to blows.

In fact the Cold War was anything but cold, with both the Soviet Union and US fighting a series of long and bloody proxy wars around the world. Ever since the Cuban missile crisis in 1962 they had been constantly testing each other's resolve on foreign battlefields. The Soviet Union also had a track record of intervening with its neighbours – it stamped out pro-democracy movements in Hungary and Czechoslovakia in 1956 and 1968 respectively, and on both occasions NATO had done nothing.

The Soviet intervention in Hungary was dubbed Operation Whirlwind. In response to calls for Soviet troops to leave the country, elements of two Soviet motor rifle divisions supported by tanks had rolled into Budapest and a further

75,000 troops streamed into the country. The Hungarian Army melted away and the revolutionaries were overwhelmed. In the fighting that followed, 3,000 Hungarians were killed. In total this invasion involved up to twelve divisions with 3,000 tanks. This was a conventional operation in which the Soviets employed the same tactics they had used during the Second World War.

In the case of Czechoslovakia, as part of Operation Danube, the 103rd Guards Air Assault Division (GAAD) arrived to seize Prague, followed by two motor rifle divisions. At the time the number of Warsaw Pact forces – including Bulgarian, East German, Hungarian and Polish units – committed to the invasion of Czechoslovakia was believed to be 250,000 troops and 2,000 tanks. This operation ran smoothly, mainly because of the minimal resistance offered by the surprised Czechs. The Soviets lost about 150 men, most as a result of accidents.

In the winter of 1979 Moscow was confident that a swift intervention in neighbouring Afghanistan to prop up the Marxist government would be a short-lived mission and probably go largely unnoticed. After all, Afghanistan was in the Soviets' backyard and they were keen to aviod Islamic militancy spilling over into the neighbouring Soviet central Asian republics.

Despite Moscow's vast and overwhelming array of military hardware, few of its troops had had any combat experience in recent years. While Soviet advisers had been posted to its client states, it was the Cuban Army that had often been called on to do Moscow's dirty work in places such as Angola and Ethiopia. Nonetheless, Moscow had every reason to be confident that it could solve this problem on its doorstep and finally win the 'Great Game' by securing dominant influence in Kabul. (All the time that India (and modern-day Pakistan) was part of the British Empire, the 'Great Game' witnessed the British and Russians compete for control of Afghanistan as it formed a buffer between their respective empires.)

The Soviet Union certainly had the military muscle to pull off an invasion of Afghanistan. Although Moscow did not commit any armoured divisions to the invasion or subsequent occupation, the airborne and five motor rifle divisions involved were equipped with a wide variety of Soviet-designed armoured fighting vehicles (AFVs).

These formations deployed the T-54, T-55, T-62, T-72 and possibly a few of the newer T-80 main battle tanks (MBTs). Initially for the invasion the Soviets only used the older T-54/55 MBTs, but between 1981 and 1982 they were slowly replaced by the T-62, whilst some T-72s were possibly later used in the reconnaissance battalions of the motor rifle divisions. No confirmation exists of the T-80 MBT seeing combat, although it undoubtedly underwent trials in Afghanistan.

Tracked self-propelled artillery consisted of the 2S1 M-1974 (122mm), 2S3 M-1973, 2S5 M-1977 (both 152mm) and 2S9 (120mm mortar). Other tracked AFVs included the ASU-85 airborne assault gun, as well as the BMP-1/2 (Boevaya Mashina

Pekhota — infantry fighting vehicle) and BMD (Boevaya Mashina Desantnaya — airborne combat vehicle). Wheeled AFVs were the BTR-60/70 armoured personnel carriers (APCs), BRMD-2 scout cars and 23mm gun trucks.

The BTR-60 was the standard Soviet amphibious eight-wheel APC of the day. The final model BTR-60PB was fully enclosed with a small turret armed with 14.5mm and 7.62mm machine guns. The BTR-60 and its successor, the BTR-70, were the standard APCs for three motor rifle regiments of a Soviet motor rifle division; the fourth was equipped with the tracked BMP-1 infantry combat vehicle. The newer BMP-2 infantry combat vehicle first saw service in Afghanistan in 1982 with the Soviet 70th Motor Rifle Brigade, which was later stationed in Kandahar.

The four-wheel BRDM-2 scout car had a similar turret to the BTR-60PB, carrying the same armament; minus the turret it was also used to carry Sagger and Spandrel anti-tank missiles and Gaskin surface-to-air missiles (although it is uncertain if the latter saw action in Afghanistan).

The airborne assault vehicles, the BMD and ASU-85, were only used by the airborne troops: principally the 105th Guards Air Assault Division followed by elements of the 103rd GAAD and the 38th Air Assault Brigade. Likewise the 2S9 airborne artillery assault vehicle entered service in 1981 and was deployed in Afghanistan with the Soviet airborne forces.

Two years later the Soviets began adding appliqué armour and smoke-grenade launchers to their tanks in an effort to combat the Mujahideen's growing proficiency with anti-tank weapons. Some of the BMPs were also fitted with appliqué armour, while some BMPs and BTR-60/70s were up-gunned with a 30mm grenade launcher designed to provide suppressive fire.

The air-portable tracked SA-4 Ganef anti-aircraft missile carrier was deployed in Kabul, while the shorter-range wheeled rocket system, the FROG-7 (Free Rocket Over Ground), was first used operationally in Afghanistan in 1985 – a case of using a sledgehammer to crack a nut!

Soviet AFVs were normally finished in dark olive-green and in some cases used a white invasion cross on their upper surfaces, a precaution usually employed when the Soviets expected to be engaging Soviet-designed armour. The cross was seen occasionally during 1979–80. In this case Moscow could not be certain that the Afghan Army's Soviet-supplied tanks would not resist the intervention. As it transpired, the Soviets were right to take these precautions. In May 1988, during the Soviet withdrawal, BTR APCs were photographed painted in the dark green but also with a very light brown camouflage, which was probably applied to other Soviet AFVs.

In the meantime, having made the decision to intervene in Afghanistan, Moscow had little inkling that it was walking into a bear trap that would entangle its forces for almost a decade.

Soviet generals in a congratulatory mood after a successful military exercise. By 1979 the Soviet Union was at the height of its power and the Soviet High Command was confident that any intervention in Afghanistan would be as short-lived as it had been in Hungary and Czechoslovakia. This was an assessment that Moscow's generals would soon learn to regret once they had tangled with 'God's Warriors'. (*Author's Collection*)

Moscow's military parades served to emphasise the Soviet Union's might. These tanks are T-72s, which at the time were state of the art. It was accepted into service in 1972 and four years later was followed by the improved T-80. However, the T-72 did not make its first public appearance until the Red Square parade of November 1977. Both tanks saw limited action in Afghanistan. (*Tim Hedden*)

Large Soviet military exercises also served to underscore Moscow's muscle. The Russian pilot of a Mi-8 gunship coordinates his attack with a T-72 tank crew. Note the twin rocket pylons – the unguided rockets could lay down a destructive hail of fire. (*Author's Collection*)

One of the Soviets' principal air defence weapons was the ZSU-23-4 self-propelled anti-aircraft gun utilising the T-54 chassis. The quadruple 23mm cannon can fire up to 1,000 rounds per minute and as a result it was often deployed in Afghanistan in a ground support role with devastating effects. (*US DoD*)

The BMP-1 (Boevaya Mashina Pekhota) infantry combat vehicle appeared in 1967 and first saw combat with the Egyptian and Syrian Armies six years later. It subsequently saw action with the Soviet Army in Afghanistan and with the Angolan, Iraqi and Libyan Armies. The small turret houses a 73mm gun and the vehicle is often mistaken for a tank. The BMP performed particularly effectively in Afghanistan's mountainous regions. These examples belong to the Polish Army. (*Graham Thompson*)

This is the newer BMP-2 produced in the late 1970s. The most notable difference was the Model 2A42 30mm cannon, which replaced the ineffectual 73mm gun. It did not appear publicly until the Red Square parade held in November 1982 – two years after the invasion of Afghanistan. (*Author's Collection*)

While the BMD-1 (Boevaya Mashina Desantnaya) airborne combat vehicle looks like a small version of the BMP, it was designed to act as a light tank for the Soviet air assault divisions. It spearheaded the Soviet invasion of Afghanistan in December 1979. Two further versions were produced but they did not appear in time to serve in Afghanistan. (*Via Author*)

The Soviet Army's main wheeled armoured personnel carrier was the 8x8 BTR-60 seen here and the BTR-70, which appeared in 1960 and 1972 respectively. A third variant, known as the BTR-80, came on the scene in 1984. All three saw extensive service in Afghanistan. (*US DoD*)

A BRDM-2 amphibious scout car on parade – note how the censors have blanked out detail that might have given the vehicle's location. Each Soviet motorised rifle division had a total of twenty-eight BRDM-2s, with twelve in the reconnaissance battalion and four each in the tank regiments. (*Author's Collection*)

These BRMD-2s are fitted with AT-5 Spandrel wire-guided anti-tank missiles that can penetrate up to 600mm of normal steel armour. (*Author's Collection*)

Area fire support at divisional level was provided by the 122mm BM-21 multiple rocket launcher known as the Grad (meaning hail). This consisted of a Ural cross-country truck fitted with a forty-round launcher. (*Via Author*)

Yet another military vehicle on parade in Moscow. This is the FROG-7 (Free Rocket Over Ground) artillery rocket system. The short-range rocket (up to 70km) was intended for battlefield support. (*Author's Collection*)

The Soviet Army had a range of self-propelled anti-aircraft missiles systems, most notable of which were the SA-4 Ganef and the SA-6 Gainful seen here; both were 1960s vintage. (*Via Author*)

The Strela-2 of SA-7 man-portable surface-to-air missile was the Soviets' key point air defence system and it saw considerable service in Afghanistan – ironically in the hands of the Mujahideen. (*US DoD*)

The one weapon system that was initially to give the Soviets a major edge over the resistance was the Mil Mi-24 Hind helicopter gunship. This heavily armoured aircraft carried a major punch, with a nose-mounted four-barrel cannon and stub wings for guided anti-tank missiles, bombs, missiles and rocket or gun pods. (*Dmitry A. Mottl*)

The Hind went into production in the early 1970s and over 1,500 had been built by 1985, with about 250 being exported; this one belongs to the Nicaraguan Air Force. (*US DoD*)

The Soviets ensured their transport helicopters also had an air assault role. The highly successful Mi-8/17 Hip appeared in the 1960s, providing a cheap alternative to gunship or attack helicopters, and was exported around the world, seeing action in countless wars, including Afghanistan. (*Author's Collection*)

The massive Mi-6 Hook heavy transport helicopter with its very distinctive wings likewise saw combat in Afghanistan. These particular examples belonged to the Polish Air Force. (*Graham Thompson*)

Soviet air power at the time was very impressive and was designed to give Moscow air supremacy over central Europe. This is a MiG-25 Foxbat interceptor, which came into service in the late 1960s. (*US DoD*)

For the invasion of Afghanistan the Soviet Air Force's ground attack aircraft, such as the Su-24 Fencer, were soon striking ground targets. This aircraft had only entered service in the mid-1970s. The Fencer was capable of carrying a wide range of air-to-ground ordnance, including various types of missiles and free-fall conventional bombs. (*US DoD*)

Chapter Two

The Bear Wakes

Essentially the invasion of Afghanistan was a rehash of Operation Danube. Airborne assault forces were tasked to swoop into Kabul, the Afghan capital, while motor rifle divisions dashed over the border to support them. The mistake Moscow made was in thinking that Afghanistan was the same as Czechoslovakia – the Afghans were certainly not going to roll over so easily.

Initially the Soviet military intervened to help a coup topple President Hafizullah Amin and install a pro-Moscow Marxist government under Babrak Karmal. Lieutenant-General Viktor Paputin flew to Kabul on 2 December 1979, followed a week later by 1,500 men (including a regiment from the 103rd Guards Air Assault Division), deployed to the strategically important Bagram air base just to the north of the capital.

Soviet advisers paralysed the Afghan Army's equipment through a programme of so-called 'winterisation'. They also persuaded the hapless President Amin, unaware that he was about to become victim of a well-planned and well-executed coup, to move to the presidential palace on the outskirts of the city on the grounds that it would be easier to defend.

The Soviets struck on 24 December 1979; Bagram was secured in five hours and the airborne troops were reinforced to 5,000 men. The key support weapons for the air assault forces were the ASU-85 assault gun and the BMD-1. Successor to the smaller and less powerful ASU-57, the ASU-85 first appeared in public in 1962 and was the principal Soviet airborne assault vehicle. Based on the P-76 amphibious tank, it has the same engine, transmission and running gear and is approximately the same weight. Designed as an assault gun and tank destroyer, it is armed with an 85mm gun, giving it some punch. Each airborne division's assault gun battalion had thirty-one of these vehicles. The newer BMD is essentially a lightweight BMP designed for use by paratroops. The pre-series BMD vehicle first appeared in 1970 and three years later an improved type – the BMD-1 Model 1973 – was produced. This was followed in 1980 by the heavily redesigned BMD-1M. There were also two support variants, designated the BMD-2. Each airborne division was issued with 320 BMDs.

The following day, on the 25th, the main Soviet force, consisting of local motor rifle divisions, crossed the border. Directed by the Soviet 40th Army HQ at Termez (now independent Uzbekistan), the 360th and 201st Motor Rifle Divisions drove on Kabul via the strategic Salang tunnel. The 357th and 66th Motor Rifle Divisions crossed the border at Kushka (now independent Turkmenistan), occupying the key city of Kandahar to the south-west and Herat to the far west.

Two days later Soviet paratroops advanced on Kabul itself, although Spetsnaz Special Forces had already secured most of the city's main administrative buildings. The Darulaman Palace was then assaulted by the airborne troops. Amin managed to gather some soldiers still loyal to him as well as part of an Afghan tank regiment and in the fighting destroyed a number of the attacking airborne vehicles. In response the paratroops successfully knocked out eight Afghan T-54 tanks. The president, his family and advisers were all killed, possibly executed by the Spetsnaz.

Despite Afghan military resistance being largely ineffective, by the New Year Soviet casualties amounted to 6,000. By mid-January 1980 the 54th Motor Rifle Division had moved into Afghanistan and the 40th Army's forward HQ was established in Kabul. The Limited Contingent Soviet Forces Afghanistan (LCSFA) numbered 85,000 men with another 30,000 just across the border. That April the Soviets signed a 'stationing of forces agreement' with the new Democratic Republic of Afghanistan's (DRA) government, leaving the LCSFA firmly in control. The country was divided into seven military commands under the de facto control of Soviet generals. The scene was set for the Soviet–Afghan War.

The following year the Soviets shifted from using unreliable Afghan Army units, to small air-mobile Soviet forces, although the Afghan commando brigades were also employed until they became too depleted by casualties. The Soviets launched their Panjsher III and IV offensives in September 1981 and the following year were again using large sweep operations employing ground forces, with Panjsher V being launched in April–May, followed by Panjsher VI in September, all of which failed to crush Ahmad Shah Massoud's troublesome guerrillas. Major large-scale operations continued throughout that year.

In 1982 Soviet deployment in Afghanistan remained largely the same, with the commitment of 95,000 men, supported by 150 aircraft and some 600 helicopters. Casualties by this stage numbered 5,000 dead and up to 10,000 wounded. In sharp contrast the Afghan Army had dropped, largely due to desertion, from 80,000 to just 25,000 men (with divisions at only battalion and brigade strength), supported by 23,000 very unreliable police and militia.

In the face of this growing security problem the LCSFA deployed three motor rifle divisions, one airborne division and one air assault brigade, totalling an impressive 115,000 men (including 10,000 Vnutrennie Voiska – members of the MVD (Ministerstvo Vnutrennikv Del, the Ministry of Internal Security), the Interior Army and KGB). By 1984 the DRA's total armed forces were estimated at just 46,000, organised in roughly the same way as they were in 1979, with an additional infantry division and a mechanised infantry brigade.

During the 1980s military helicopters really came of age in terms of close air support (CAS) and counter-insurgency (COIN) operations. Soviet air power played a fundamental role in the Soviet Union's operations in Afghanistan between 1979 and 1989 and there can be little doubt that the cutting edge of the Soviet presence was the helicopter. In particular, transport helicopters enabled Soviet forces to penetrate deep into the Afghan mountains, whilst gunships provided swift and devastating firepower with a mix of machine guns, bombs, missiles and rocket pods. The latter was a weapon the Mujahideen soon learned to fear.

Indeed the Mi-24 Hinds conducted many of the CAS missions, while the Mi-8 Hip, supported by the larger M-6 Hook, conducted most of the troop-carrying and resupply missions. The first reported use of Soviet anti-tank helicopters came in Afghanistan in 1979 when Mi-24s knocked out Afghan tanks around the presidential palace in Kabul. Within a very short time the Soviets had some 600 helicopters, including 200 Mi-24s, supporting operations in Afghanistan.

An elderly Afghan tribesman sits high in the Hindu Kush. His weapon is an ancient lever-action rifle. Afghanistan was for a long time a pawn in the rivalry between the expanding British and Russian Empires. Despite Britain's withdrawal from India in 1948 the Soviets felt they had unfinished business in Afghanistan. (*Author's Collection*)

Afghanistan was and still is a land of very stark contrasts between the medieval simplicity of rural life and a more cosmopolitan urban middle class. This crowd of youngsters was photographed on the streets of Kabul just before the Soviet invasion. (*Via Author*)

Soviet ASU-85 airborne assault guns of the 103rd Guards Air Assault Division were airlifted into Bagram air base outside Kabul. Just prior to the Soviet motor rifle divisions rolling over the border the Soviets expanded their airborne strength in the Afghan city during early December 1979. (*Author's Collection*)

A Soviet Mi-8 Hip helicopter comes in to land at Bagram air base – the initial Soviet deployment was only 1,500 men, but this rapidly rose to 5,000 with elements from three divisions. (*Author's Collection*)

Battle is commenced. The first the Afghans knew of the invasion was the sight of Soviet air assault BMD-1 airborne combat vehicles on the road south from Bagram heading for Kabul. This young crewman seems to be in quite good spirits; little did he know that he was embarking on a ten-year conflict. (*US DoD*)

A BMD-1 on the streets of Kabul. The Soviets secured Bagram on 24 December 1979 and three days later moved into the capital. A two-battalion attack by BMD-mounted paratroops swiftly took the Duralaman Palace and killed Afghan President Amin. (*US DoD*)

A Soviet crew sit atop their BTR armoured personnel carrier having helped secure Kabul. (*Igor Bondarets*)

Soviet airborne troops posing for the camera somewhere outside Kabul; they are armed with the AK-74 assault rifle – the invasion was spearheaded by elements of the 103rd, 104th and 105th Guards Air Assault Divisions. (*Author's Collection*)

T-62 tanks roll into Afghanistan. On 25 December 1979 four Soviet motor rifle divisions crossed the border. Two divisions were to support the Soviet airborne forces and they moved on Kabul via the Salang tunnel. (*Via Author*)

The strategically vital Salang tunnel which cuts through the mountains to the north of Kabul was to be the scene of many ambushes in the years to come. (*Via Author*)

Tank transporters rumble through the streets. These Soviet tanks are being moved up on low loaders to avoid wear and tear on the tracks. The Soviet Army quickly secured control of Afghanistan's key towns; it was in the mountains that the problems began to occur. (*US DoD*)

A column of T-54s – this was the most numerous type of tank serving with the Soviet motor rifle divisions that invaded Afghanistan and serving with the Afghan Army. (*US DoD*)

Slavic and central Asian Soviet airborne troops are briefed on their mission – note the BMD on the right. The four motor rifle divisions were bolstered with Soviet central Asians, especially Tajiks, to make it look as if they were going to help the Afghan government rather than take over the country. (*Igor Bondarets*)

Soviet troops horse around in the Afghan snows outside their barracks block – it would not be long before they were facing fierce resistance, especially in Kunar (to the north of the Khyber Pass) and Paktia provinces. (*Author's Collection*)

Soviet BMP and MTLB infantry combat vehicles in Afghanistan. The BMP-1 is armed with a 73mm cannon and could also carry Sagger anti-tank missiles that were used in Afghanistan for house busting. Amongst the most successful of post-Second World War infantry fighting vehicles, the BMP appeared in 1967. (*Author's Collection*)

A Soviet BTR APC passes a BMP-1. The BTR-60PB and its successor, the BTR-70, constituted the most numerous Soviet armoured vehicles deployed to Afghanistan. Soviet motorised rifle units were heavily employed on convoy duty, using such trusted vehicles as these. The earlier BTR-60P entered service with the Soviet Army in 1961 and has since been supplied in a variety of models. (*Igor Bondarets*)

The historic Khyber Pass is one of the two main routes through the mountains from Pakistan into Afghanistan. In southern Pakistan the road runs from the city of Quetta to Chaman through the Khojak Pass across the border up to Kandahar, which sits astride Afghanistan's great ring road. To the north the road runs from Islamabad through Peshawar to the Khyber Pass and over the border to Jalalabad and on to Kabul. (*Author's Collection*)

The BMP-2 is armed with a 30mm cannon rather than the ineffectual 73mm. The chassis is almost identical to the earlier BMP-1 but has additional armour protection and the commander is positioned in the turret instead of sitting behind the driver. Over the years 550 BMP-1/2s have been supplied to Afghanistan. (*Via Author*)

These Russian or Ukrainian soldiers are leaning against what looks like an up-armoured T-62E main battle tank. (*Igor Bondarets*)

MiG-21s, MiG-23s (seen here) and MiG-27s were committed to the air war in Afghanistan. (*US DoD*)

This is what greeted the Soviet and Afghan armies in the foothills and mountains: armed defiance. Afghanistan's tough tribal fighters had spent decades resisting the authority of Kabul – in the rural areas the Soviets were not wanted or welcome. (*IAAM*)

Chapter Three

Kabul's Armour

The Democratic Republic of Afghanistan's armour was really a poorer cousin to the Soviets' armoured units, particularly their tank battalions. Equipped with older vehicles and deemed unreliable, they were often relegated to static guard duties – particularly in Kabul and the other major cities, where they still managed to cause trouble. In 1979 the Afghan Army fielded some 860 tanks and 400 APCs, with four armoured divisions consisting of the 14th (which mutinied in Ghazni in July 1980), whilst the 4th, 7th and 15th were really only of brigade strength.

The DRA was equipped with the Second World War vintage T-34/85, plus T-54, T-55 and T-62 MBTs, BTR-152/60 APCs, BMP-1 infantry combat vehicles and BRDM-2 scout cars. The rather old six-wheel BTR-152, capable of carrying up to seventeen infantrymen, had been withdrawn from frontline service with the Soviet Army, but continued to be used by Afghan military units. The BTR-60s and 152s could transport only about one-third of the DRA's infantry, while the BMPs were limited to supporting the armoured brigades.

The T-54s and T-55s were used in the DRA's armoured units, the T-34/85s as infantry support and the T-62s were mainly stationed around the capital. The DRA's T-62 force was usually based at Pul-e-Charki, the site of a notorious prison near Kabul. During the invasion the Soviets immobilised them by removing the batteries for 'winterisation' storage. One DRA tank regiment that remained operational lost eight tanks whilst defending the Darulaman Palace against the Soviet attack.

For air defence both the DRA and the Soviets deployed the anti-aircraft (AA) 23mm ZSU-23-4 self-propelled gun, which on occasions was used in a direct ground support role. DRA AFVs were also finished in the Soviet drab green, with similar white tactical numbers; as DRA insignia were not displayed on AFVs in the field it was often very difficult to tell DRA and Soviet armour apart. Not that the Mujahideen were worried by such distinctions – as far as they were concerned an enemy tank was an enemy tank.

In 1979 the Afghan military had an impressive strength – on paper – of 80,000 in the army, organised into ten infantry divisions supported by the four armoured divisions, an artillery brigade, three mountain infantry brigades, three artillery and two commando regiments. The army could also draw on 150,000 reservists. The air force numbered about 10,000, equipped with 169 combat aircraft, with another 12,000 reservists. The gendarmerie fielded about 30,000 police and militiamen equipped with small arms.

The Afghan Army's response to the Soviet intervention was mixed and many units were unable or unwilling to resist, although the 8th Afghan Division fought, and lost 2,000 men for its trouble. On the whole most Afghan units whose loyalty to the government was questionable were simply disarmed and the army's manpower dropped by 50 per cent. The Soviets also relieved the Afghan Army of its anti-tank and anti-aircraft missiles in 1980 when a great deal of equipment disappeared with deserters.

Loyalty was a constant problem. For example, in 1983 some fifty-two Afghan Air Force and seventy-nine Army personnel were arrested for collaborating with an attack on Shindand air base, in which seven MiG jets and thirty tanks were blown up. These arrests resulted in the desertion of over 300 Afghan troops. Further problems were experienced at Shindand in June 1985: Afghan pilots blew up twenty aircraft after the execution of three pilots who had jettisoned their bombs rather than hit a village.

Throughout the war the DRA Army suffered a continual drain in manpower due to desertion. After the invasion it dropped to just 32,000 and by 1985 could still only muster at best 40,000 men; it had an annual loss of 10,000 men through failure to answer the call-up, desertion, disease and combat casualties. Nonetheless constant tank replacements by the Soviet Union meant that Kabul's tank fleet remained at about 300 T-54/55s and T-62s.

In 1981 the Mujahideen captured a BMP-1 from the DRA's 7th Armoured Brigade and its crew sometimes took it into action alongside the guerrillas. On 10 September 1983 the seven-man crew of an APC fitted with AA guns, probably a ZSU-23-4, from Spin Boldak camp near the Pakistani border, came over to the Mujahideen along with their vehicle.

T-55A '517', captured in Paktia province in 1983, saw limited action with the Mujahideen. Along with two other tanks in December 1983 it was used unsuccessfully to attack the town of Urgun. During the Soviet withdrawal increasing numbers of tanks and AFVs began to fall into their hands, as the outlying towns were abandoned. The Mujahideen often daubed their captured vehicles with graffiti and religious slogans.

By the mid-1980s the DRA Air Force was down to 7,000 men with 150 combat aircraft and thirty helicopters, while the unreliable paramilitary forces still stood at 30,000. All army units were under strength, with divisions really equating to little more than brigades; this decline continually forced the LCSFA to expand its role

(NATO faced exactly the same problem in Afghanistan decades later) and conduct most of the fighting.

In 1988 US intelligence sources estimated that the DRA armed forces had risen to 150,000, though less than 20,000 were considered to be reliable. In reality the army consisted of some 50,000 reluctant conscripts, equipped with 450 predominantly T-54 tanks, supported by an air force of 5,000 with around 100 MiGs, some 70,000 KHAD (Khadamat-e Aettla'at-e Dawlat – State Intelligence Agency) forces and regional militias of over 100,000.

An Afghan soldier on guard somewhere in Kabul wearing the standard-issue heavy woollen winter uniform and greatcoat; note the studded belt. Rather than resist the Soviet invasion many Afghan recruits simply deserted. (*US DoD*)

More Afghan soldiers photographed in Kabul; they were ill equipped and poorly motivated. Their fixed bayonets indicate they are also on guard duty, despite sitting down on the job. Most of them had little desire to fight for the government and its Soviet allies against their own people. (*US DoD*)

The bulk of the Afghan Army's armoured forces were equipped with the old T-54/55. The 12.7mm heavy machine gun mounted on this tank for anti-aircraft duties proved very popular with the Mujahideen. (*Graham Thompson*)

Another T-55 (this one actually belongs to the Polish Army); in 1979 the Afghan Army had around 500 of these tanks, though its inventory also included T-34s, T-62s and PT-76s. (*Graham Thompson*)

As well as artillery the Afghan Army also fielded the 122mm Grad BM-21 multiple-rocket launcher. (*Author's Collection*)

In 1985 the Soviet Army started using the FROG-7b against Afghan villages harbouring the Mujahideen. A few years later around a dozen launchers and time-expired rounds from Soviet stocks were supplied to the Afghan Army. (*Via Author*)

An Afghan soldier in winter uniform, equipped with the Soviet RPD light machine gun. The belt buckle is also Soviet pattern. (*AIO/Julian Gearing*)

The look of uncertainty on this Afghan soldier's face says it all – poor morale and desertion were major problems throughout the Soviet–Afghan War. (*AIO/Julian Gearing*)

Afghan troops or militia fraternising with a Soviet BTR APC crew. Behind the scenes Moscow had little faith in the Afghan Army's fighting qualities or indeed loyalty. (*Igor Bondarets*)

While the Soviets were generous in supplying military equipment to the Afghan government forces, they only gave them the older-generation tanks such as the T-55 (seen here) and T-62; newer T-62M, T-64, T-72 and T-80 were never supplied. (*Author's Collection*)

Mujahideen pose with a tank from another age – The T-34/85 was a veteran of the Second World War. However, at the time of the Soviet invasion Kabul had about 200 of these tanks still in service. (*AIO/Julian Gearing*)

Soviet soldiers preparing to move out with their BTR armoured personnel carriers. They are clearly a mixture of Slavic and central Asian recruits. Despite Soviet support and weapons, from the very start the Afghan government forces found it difficult to find a successful response to the politico-religious appeal of the Mujahideen waging jihad against the invaders from the north. (*Igor Bondarets*)

A soviet photograph of Afghan troops plodding past a stationary convoy. They are armed with the AKM assault rifle – the newer version of the AK-47. When isolated Afghan and Soviet army garrisons could not be resupplied by air then convoys had to be pushed through to them, which inevitably invited attack. (*Via Author*)

This convoy of petrol tankers suffered such a fate; by the time the Soviet relief force got to them it was too late. The Soviet Army did not like being tied to convoy duty and often left it to the Afghan Army to ride shotgun – the Soviets saw it as their job to provide the rapid reaction force with which to take on the attackers. (*Via Author*)

Rusting Grad rocket launchers; the tubes can fire forty rockets in a variety of combinations. (*US DoD*)

Soviet BTRs undergoing engine maintenance somewhere in Afghanistan. (*Igor Bondarets*)

The MiG-17 and MiG-21 (seen here) provided the backbone of the Afghan Air Force. In 1979 they had eighty and thirty-five of these aircraft respectively. (*Author's Collection*)

The Afghans were also equipped with the older Fitter Su-17. Both Soviet and Afghan Sukhois were heavily engaged throughout the Soviet–Afghan War in their intended air-to-ground role. (*US DoD*)

This group of resistance fighters clearly includes Afghan Army deserters. Note the man at the back in the cap is still wearing his uniform. Thanks to tribal loyalties, desertion remained a problem throughout the war. (*Abdul Malik Garvin*)

Chapter Four

Mujahideen – God's Warriors

After the invasion the Afghan countryside was initially reasonably quiet, but during the spring and summer of 1980 fierce resistance began to escalate in Kunar and Paktia provinces. Increasing numbers of Afghans took to the mountains, with opposition growing in the eastern and north-eastern valleys and, to a lesser extent, to the west.

By mid-year the Soviets had begun to systematically destroy Afghanistan's agriculture in a move designed to depopulate the rural communities and deny the rebels safe haven. In September they launched their first offensive against the Mujahideen stronghold in the northern Panjsher valley, which juts into the Hindu Kush mountain range, just 96km north of Kabul. This area was held by the Jamiat-i-Islami (Islamic Society), a moderate fundamentalist group led by a Tajik former engineering student named Ahmad Shah Massoud.

Eventually, after a series of such offensives, Massoud held a controversial ceasefire with the Soviets, in part because of in-fighting amongst the various guerrilla factions. This came to an end in April 1984 when the Panjsher VII offensive launched 10,000 Soviet and 1,500 Afghan troops against his fighters. Panjsher VIII followed in September 1984.

Although the Soviets were fighting the war on the cheap and at an acceptable level in terms of costs and casualties, by 1984 the Afghan government had no control over 85 per cent of the countryside, with guerrilla attacks almost a daily occurrence everywhere. There was an increasing use of Soviet heliborne forces and the brutal air war continued against the helpless rural population. However, Massoud's forces still remained in control of the Panjsher even after the Soviets' IX offensive, and the Mujahideen began to stand and fight for the first time.

Crude Afghan Marxist policy and Soviet counter-insurgency tactics, such as destroying crops and terrorising civilians, led to hundreds of thousands of people fleeing their homes: into neighbouring Iran to the west and Pakistan to the east. Afghanistan ended up with some 3 million internal refugees living in the cities and countryside. By mid-1987 there were an additional 3 million registered and an estimated 400,000 unregistered refugees in Pakistan. This huge pool of people provided an ideal sanctuary and recruiting ground for the Mujahideen. Iran was thought to have 2.5 million Afghan refugees, but was less flexible about their cross-border movements, hampering guerrilla operations.

The number of Mujahideen who fought jihad or 'holy war' against the Soviets and the DRA is difficult to estimate. In 1984 the resistance forces were assessed to be around 90,000, of whom only 20,000 were active fighters supported by fifteen exiled political groups. Later figures vary from 130,000 to half a million, though by the late 1980s the Mujahideen were thought to number about 150,000, with 40,000 active guerrillas supported by 110,000 reserves; certainly the vast majority of the rural population supported the rebels.

There were seven major resistance organisations with their HQ in Peshawar in Pakistan, consisting of:

Mohaz Milli Islami (National Islamic Front of Afghanistan) operated in Kandahar, Badakhshan, Ghanzi, Warduk and Kabul areas.

Jebhe Mille Nejad (National Liberation Front of Sibghtullah Modjaddidi) operated in the Jalalabad, Logar and Kandahar areas.

Harakat-i-Inquilabi-i-Islami (Islamic Revolutionary Movement of Mohammed Nadi Mohammed) had widespread support in Ghanzi, Wardak, Koh-i-Safi, Badakshan and Kunar regions.

Hezbi-i-Islami (Islamic Party of Younis Khalsi) was strong in Kabul, Nangarhar and Paktika provinces.

Jamiat-i-Islami (Islamic Society of Professor Burhanuddin Rabbani) was active in Herat, Mazar-e-Sharif, Badakshan, Takhar Parwan and Kapisa provinces.

Ittehad-e-Islami (Islamic Alliance of Professor Abdul Rasoul Sayeff) was active mainly in the Paghman region.

Hezbi-e-Islami (Islamic Party of Gulbuddin Hekmatayr) operated mainly on the Pathan areas.

Mujahideen weapons consisted largely of Soviet-designed small arms that came from a variety of sources; heavy equipment was limited mainly to infantry support weapons. Although highly successful at guerrilla warfare and able to stand and fight when the need arose, the Mujahideen were hampered by their inability to counter the Soviets' helicopter gunships effectively due to insufficient numbers of accurate man-portable SAMs. This problem was not resolved until 1986 when US Stinger became more readily available.

Known as the 'Dashika' by the Mujahideen, the Soviet 12.7mm DShKM heavy machine gun saw extensive action with the rebels in Afghanistan against Soviet helicopters flying nap-of-the-earth operations. The Soviet- and Chinese-made versions of the Dashika along with the 'Ziqroiat' ZPU-1/ZGU-1 14.5mm were the Mujahideen's standard air-defence weapons. Above the deafening whine of the rotors a pilot and his co-pilot probably could not hear the 'clunk-clunk-clunk' of the machine gun firing in at them. What they must have felt was the impact of the heavy rounds striking the side of their helicopter.

Certainly Soviet helicopters did not have it all their own way and had to quickly adopt low level nap-of-the-earth techniques, as Mi-24s were reportedly lost to Mujahideen armed with SA-7 SAMs as early as 1980. Surprisingly the Pakistanis even claimed to have shot down an Afghan Hind-A, straying over the border, with a quad machine gun. Whilst only two dozen helicopters had been lost by 1983, the growing use of infrared heat-seeking missiles by the resistance was to be the death knell for Soviet helicopter supremacy.

In the first six months of 1986 Soviet and Afghan government forces lost 105 helicopters, compared to a six-monthly average of forty the previous year. These casualties reportedly brought total helicopter losses in Afghanistan up to 500, though such a figure is impossible to verify. Over the years some Afghan Mi-8s also defected to the Mujahideen, though most were simply stripped of their weapons.

The Mujahideen were unable to field large numbers of vehicles, although they captured some wheeled and tracked AFVs in the eastern provinces, but their use was limited by the lack of fuel, ammunition and the threat of Soviet air strikes. Jeeps seem to have been particularly popular amongst the guerrillas. On the whole, though, captured AFVs were simply cannibalised of all useful weapons, particularly machine guns, which could be used for air defence. Pack animals such as horses, mules and camels were the preferred modes of transport when it came to moving weapons and ammunition through the mountains.

(*Opposite, bottom*) A gathering of Mujahideen posing for the camera armed with AK-47 and G3 assault rifles, SKS carbines and rocket-propelled grenades. (*Erwin Franzen*)

A group of Afghans attending a *shura* or council. The Soviet Army's arrival was initially greeted largely with indifference but soon escalated to open hostility once Soviet forces pushed out into the provinces. (*US DoD*)

Guns flooded over the Pakistani border, many of them obsolete, including 100,000 ancient British Lee-Enfield rifles which came from old Indian Army stocks. (*Via Author*)

Resistance fighters proudly display their AK-47 assault rifles and RPG just before a raid. In reality the assault rifles are almost certainly Type 56, the Chinese copy of the Soviet Kalashnikov. (*Erwin Franzen*)

Commander Shapoor and three of his men from the Yunus Khalis group preparing for a rocket attack on Barikot garrison in Kunar province in August 1985. The fighter at the back is holding an RPG-7, while the man in the foreground is cradling a Type 56 assault rifle. (*Erwin Franzen*)

Afghan children with the Soviet-designed 14.5mm anti-aircraft gun in Kunar in October 1987. This weapon was greatly favoured by the Mujahideen. (*Erwin Franzen*)

Guerrilla gunners proudly show off their anti-aircraft gun – this is a captured ZPU-1 14.5mm anti-aircraft gun based on the Soviet KPV machine gun. It is mounted on a two-wheeled carriage that can be dismantled into several 80kg pieces for easy transport, which was ideal for the Afghan mountains. The Mujahideen also made use of the ZPU-2 and ZPU-4, which are two- and four-barrel versions. (*Julian Gearing*)

At the start of the Soviet–Afghan War the resistance relied on the 'Dashika' or 12.7mm DShKM heavy machine gun for air defence. These were capable of bringing down transport helicopters. (*Via Author*)

The Soviet SA-7 Grail was the resistance's only surface-to-air missile until the arrival of the American Stinger and the British Blowpipe. Some SA-7s were captured from the Afghan Army, while the Palestinian Liberation Organisation and Egypt supplied others. Not an easy-to-use 'soldier-proof' weapon, it was never available in great numbers. (*US DoD*)

A typical group of Mujahideen photographed in Kunar province in 1985. The men at the front are armed with the ubiquitous Kalashnikov assault rifle, while those behind are sporting heavier machine guns. (*IAAM/Jonas Dovydenas*)

Resistance leader Ahmad Shah Massoud is brandishing an AKS-74 with a BG-15 grenade launcher. These were carried by Soviet heliborne troops, along with RPG-18 and RPG-22 light anti-tank weapons and RPO-A Shmel single-shot flame rockets, to increase their firepower. Clearly it did its first owner no good. (AIO/Julian Gearing)

Journalist Erwin Franzen poses with an AKMS Kalashnikov assault rifle in Jaji in the summer of 1984. (*Erwin Franzen*)

A group of resistance fighters during a lull in the fighting; they are all wearing the Pakistani *pakol* cap which became a distinctive trademark of the rebels. (*AIO/Julian Gearing*)

Mujahideen in Munda Dir district communicating by radio with comrades fighting in Kunar in 1985. (*Erwin Franzen*)

This could be a Chinese Type 69 or Soviet-made RPG-7. The resistance used it as an all-purpose support weapon. (*US DoD*)

Captured rockets – the Mujahideen tended to use these in place of artillery to bombard military bases and air fields. (*US DoD*)

Captured Soviet field guns in Jaji, Paktia in August 1984. (*Erwin Franzen*)

These guerrilla fighters are preparing for a mission. The weapon on the tripod is a Chinese-supplied 107mm rocket; lacking artillery the Mujahideen used these to pound targets. (*IAAM*)

Like father, like son: this Mujahideen is teaching his boy about jihad through passages in the Koran. His personal weapon is the Soviet RPK light machine gun, immediately identifiable by the wooden paddle-shaped butt stock. (*Abdul Malik Garvin*)

Despite the presence of the pickup and lorry, most Afghan villages such as this one had not changed greatly since the Middle Ages. The Afghans were happy with their lot and had no desire to change – in the face of such stubbornness the Soviet Air Force sought to depopulate the countryside, thereby herding everyone into the cities or refugee camps. (*Abdul Malik Garvin*)

Chapter Five

Tank Killers

Despite the Soviet Army and the DRA government forces possessing superior armoured firepower, Afghanistan's geography never favoured armoured combat and its conduct was invariably to the detriment of the Communist forces involved.

Despite a lack of heavy anti-tank guns the Mujahideen were able to exact a significant toll on the DRA/Soviet armoured units. Afghanistan soon became littered with such rusting casualties. Their main anti-tank weapon of choice was the Soviet or Chinese-copy rocket-propelled grenade (RPG). Mujahid Hamid Walid, one of the guerrillas' best RPG-7 gunners personally knocked out twelve AFVs and numerous trucks. Walid, who always wore a black Soviet aircrew helmet into action, was killed on 23 July 1983 whilst engaging a Soviet convoy on the Ghanzi highway.

Much cruder methods were resorted to, including Molotov cocktails and home-made bombs. A trick the Mujahideen employed was to dig a deep trench across a narrow mountain road and then cover it. Once the lead tank had fallen in, blocking the way, the Mujahideen would then smear mud over the tank's driver slits before dousing the vehicle in petrol. The crew then had the option of sitting tight and hoping the flames did not take hold or bailing out to face inevitable death. The guerrillas also became adept at customising very large anti-tank mines.

Mujahideen courage seemed to have no limit when tackling enemy armoured vehicles. Throughout the war both the DRA and Soviets lost large numbers of AFVs, with losses continually increasing. The Mujahideen excelled in ambushing and trapping convoys. In the Panjsher valley – site of numerous Soviet offensives – on the road from Sangana to Khenji the Mujahideen ambushed a big convoy, which included four T-55s, over a dozen BTR-60s and fifteen lorries, some of which plunged into the river bordering the road. In Khenji itself an abandoned tank, an APC, several lorries and a DRA Army mess truck were all testimony to the ferocity of the attack.

In May–June 1982 half a dozen Soviet BTR-60s were knocked out and a tank ended up stranded in the middle of the river by guerrillas armed with RPGs at Shawa, halfway up the Panjsher valley. Also a T-72 reportedly had its turret blown off by a home-made mine at Bazarak. The year 1983 represented a typical period of continual harassment and ambushes: during June–December the Mujahideen accounted for about 273 AFVs.

A brief survey illustrates the constant drain the DRA/Soviet armoured formations suffered as well as the large number of ambush actions fought. Mujahideen and collaborating DRA Air Force and Army personnel blew up thirty tanks in June 1983 at Shindand air base. Between July and August 14 Soviet tanks were destroyed in Farah province, while in August an attack on a Soviet military post at Chakri south-east of Kabul saw two tanks damaged and a garrison of eighty massacred. Also during August 1983 a further two tanks were knocked out in Kandahar province.

Between 3 August and 3 September 1983 the Mujahideen attacked a convoy seven times during its passage through Logar en route for Paktia province, destroying thirteen AFVs, thirty-two trucks and six oil tankers. Another convoy, 2,000 vehicles strong, passing through Hairtan Port to Khuln, was attacked on 18 August when crossing the Soviet/Afghan border over a newly constructed bridge across the Amu Darya river, losing two tanks and a jeep. The convoy continued to advance with helicopter gunships flying cover, but they failed to disperse the guerrillas; two more tanks and several vehicles had to be abandoned later after being set alight. Other clashes in the province accounted for a further five tanks at Khullam and Samahan.

In 1985 the Mujahideen six-month kill average was 180 tanks and 530 other vehicles; during the first six months of 1986 DRA/Soviet forces lost 380 tanks and 1,120 other vehicles, representing a considerable increase. A major armoured operation was launched in the spring of 1986, when 2,000 AFVs pushed out of Khost in an effort to lift the siege. In July 1986 the Soviets proposed to withdraw six regiments – some 8,000 men – as a sign of goodwill towards the general withdrawal negotiations. In October 1986 the forces withdrawn included one tank regiment, which had only recently been brought up to strength with T-72s, three anti-aircraft regiments (which had no tactical value) and two motorised rifle regiments.

The brown rusting hulk of a DRA or Soviet AFV, usually stripped bare, marked every mountain pass, road, gully and riverbed. The Mujahideen were frequently photographed standing triumphantly like big game hunters on top of their latest victim. Afghanistan became an AFV graveyard with so much scrap metal.

The battle that probably saw the most AFVs knocked out in one operation was the relief of Khost, fought during November–December 1987. In the dogged fighting that saw the temporary lifting of the siege, the Mujahideen claimed to have destroyed some 110 AFVs, including forty-seven tanks.

By 1987–88, even though suffering continual losses, the DRA (with Soviet supplies) still managed to retain a powerful armoured force, consisting of 300 T-54/55, 100 T-62, 50 T-34, 400 BTR and 40 BMP. The majority of the Soviet AFVs deployed in Afghanistan, such as the MBTs and large rocket launchers, proved to be ungainly and virtually useless against the guerrilla ambush tactics of the Mujahideen. Ultimately, though, the critical difference was not in the hardware but in the endurance of both sides.

This guerrilla is evidently a full-time RPG operator as the pack on his back is for spare grenades. He is wearing a Soviet tank crew helmet, which was probably a trophy from one of his kills. The RPG-7 anti-tank grenade launcher, both Soviet- and Chinese-made, along with mines, were the Mujahideen's main anti-tank weapons. (*IAAM*)

A resistance anti-tank team conducting an ambush. (*AIO/Julian Gearing*)

An Afghan guerrilla with a captured Soviet 80mm RPG-22 disposable anti-tank rocket launcher. Along with the 66mm RPG-18, these were never as popular or as successfull as the older RPG-7. (*AIO/Julian Gearing*)

Mujahideen children in Kunar province in August 1985. The little boy is holding a grenade reload for a RPG. (*Erwin Franzen*)

This Soviet tank clearly ran into trouble – a knocked-out or abandoned T-55 covered in Afghan fighters. The Mujahideen rarely took captured tanks back into battle. (*Author's Collection*)

Another tank-killer squad, comprising two RPG gunners, their assistants with the reloads and their armed escort. (*Erwin Franzen*)

An Afghan guerrilla being trained with the RGP-7 anti-tank grenade launcher. The grenade has four fins that flick out when fired, which helped stabilise it in flight. (*IAAM*)

These Soviet gunners are posing with their 2S3 (M-1973) 152mm self-propelled howitzer. Their coats indicate it is late in the year. This powerful weapon system entered service with the Soviet Army in 1971 and was deployed at a rate of eighteen per tank division or motorised rifle division (fielded with six guns per battery, with three batteries making up a regiment). (*Igor Bondarets*)

The face of the guerrilla war. Afghan fighters pose atop a captured Soviet BTR-60; rather unusually they are not holding any weapons. (*Via Author*)

A knocked-out BTR-60 somewhere in Oruzgan province. Such abandoned vehicles became commonplace throughout Afghanistan. (*US DoD*)

Two young Soviet motor rifle troops in tropical uniform in front of a BTR armoured personnel carrier. While this vehicle provided good general protection for transporting men and their equipment, it was not immune to RPGs and mines. (*Igor Bondarets*)

This Soviet convoy of BTR and BMP armoured personnel carriers has come to a halt while the crews stop for a cigarette break. The relaxed manner of this man and the lack of personal weapons indicate that this photo was taken within the security of a base perimeter where attack was not expected. (*Igor Bondarets*)

More Soviet BTRs being used to make a tent to shade out the midday heat. The raised hatches normally cover the engine. (*Igor Bondarets*)

Soviets chatting by a BMP with the rear doors flung open – while they look in good cheer, being closed up inside any AFVs was hellishly hot during the summer. (*Igor Bondarets*)

Mujahideen with ancient bolt-action Enfield rifles and an RPG-7. They were photographed on their way to Saohol Sar pass, Kunar province, in the summer of 1985. (*Erwin Franzen*)

Another rusting hulk blotting the Afghan landscape – in this case a long-abandoned T-55 tank. (*US DoD*)

The Soviet T-72 was introduced into Afghanistan in the early 1980s with reconnaissance battalions of the motor rifle divisions. About the only way the Mujahideen could knock these tanks out was by using heavy-duty mines. (*US DoD*)

Resistance fighters and a European journalist pose on top of a disabled Afghan/Soviet tank. If a cameraman was about, such posing was a regular pastime for the Mujahideen. (*IAAM*)

Soviet armoured vehicles captured by the Mujahideen – they consist of a BTR-60 armoured personnel carrier and a BRDM-2 armoured car. (*Via Author*)

Chapter Six

The Convoy War

The lack of any rail system in Afghanistan limited the movement of supplies to air and road transport, as well as pipelines – all of which were vulnerable to attack. The primary Soviet air workhorse was the Ilyushin 76 (Il-76) 'Candid'. The Soviet Military Transport Aviation (Voyenno Transportnaya Aviatsi – VTA) had a fleet of 577 aircraft, of which 385 were the tried and trusted Il-76. It has a maximum payload of forty tonnes, 140 soldiers or 125 paratroopers, with a maximum range of 4,600km.

On the ground Soviet general-purpose vehicle cargo carriers consisted of the 6x6 Ural-375, 6x4 Ural-377 and Zil-131 trucks. There were also tanker versions of the Ural-375 and the Zil. The Maz-537 provided tractor-trailer lift for the heavy equipment such as tanks and armoured personnel carriers.

The Soviets soon found that the Mujahideen could easily withdraw in the face of their mechanised sweeps. As a result they required more helicopters for greater tactical mobility, more air support and improved air-dropped anti-personnel weapons.

Soviet convoy protection became increasingly professional, with helicopters offering rapid suppressive fire or inserting flanking troops in response to attacks. Air munitions such as the deadly plastic PFM-1 butterfly mine were dropped in huge quantities by helicopter in order to disrupt guerrilla supply lines and block their escape routes.

By the second half of 1981 the Soviet armed forces were using a new co-ordinated all-arms (backed by close air support (CAS)) style of counter-insurgency tactics. This emphasised the concentration of air assets, extensive preliminary bombardment and landing heliborne forces to block and engage the enemy from unexpected directions – followed by a fully mechanised push, usually towards a pre-positioned heliborne blocking force.

Rebel attacks with the assistance of the Pakistani Inter-Service Intelligence (ISI) expanded in the important Paktia province bordering Pakistan in mid-1983. Under an ex-Afghan Army colonel, Ramatullah Safi, the Mohaz Melli Islami (National Islamic Front of Afghanistan) began to launch major raids during the summer and autumn. About 5,000 Mujahideen moved into the bazaar area of Khost in August. The following month they occupied Matun and Khurhai in the same area and most of the local militia surrendered. The result was that 300 Soviet and 1,500 Afghan troops were trapped in the town of Khost. By occupying the bazaar areas of Khost, Jaji (also called Ali Khel) and Urgana, the guerrillas were able to bring large quantities of arms, routed through the ISI, directly over the Pakistani border by truck instead of by pack animal.

In three days of fierce fighting during that summer the Mujahideen failed to capture Khost, but knocked out eight tanks and five armoured personnel carriers; 220 PoWs from the Gul Ghundi, Khost and Urgun also surrendered after garrison life became intolerable. The Afghan 37th Commando Brigade subsequently reinforced Khost, which protected the Bati Pass into Pakistan.

The significance of Khost was not lost on the DRA government. The Afghan minister of defence, political commissar of the army and the military commander of the south-eastern region all flew into Khost by helicopter, pledging greater assistance for the beleaguered garrison. The Mujahideen again made their presence known around Khost on 15 October 1983 when they shot down two Soviet transport aircraft trying to land. The situation, though, was considered stable enough for the 37th Commando to be airlifted out.

'By 1985 the Mujahideen leaders and senior commanders were determined Khost should fall,' recalled Brigadier Mohammad Yousaf, head of the Pakistani ISI's Afghan Bureau supporting the Mujahideen, 'and a major offensive was mooted to this end. To take a strongly-held town such as Khost was not really a task for a guerrilla force.'

At the same time, having failed to defeat the Mujahideen in the field, the Soviets tried to strangle their vital supply routes, and in mid-1985 attempted to halt the flow of arms from Pakistan as well as relieve Barikot (which had been under siege since 1981). By June a Soviet-led force of about 4,000 troops had succeeded in forcing the Mujahideen to withdraw.

This increased guerrilla activity in the Khost area resulted in a major offensive in August–September 1985 involving 10,000 Soviet troops spearheaded by Spetsnaz Special Forces and 10,000 Afghan soldiers. They succeeded in driving the Hezbi-i-Islaml (Islamic Party) under Jalulladin Haqani from the bazaar, but failed to break the siege or take the Mujahideen border stronghold of Zhawar. Ominously, by December there were 10,000 Mujahideen in the Khost area.

Brigadier Yousaf fretted over how best to defeat the Soviets: 'Throughout mid-1985 I did much soul-searching as to whether my overall strategy was working. Our efforts to keep the enemy away from the border areas seemed to have failed, we had suffered casualties, our attempt to seize Khost had been badly flawed, and the Soviet high command had apparently gained the initiative.'

That year saw some of the most intensive fighting of the war. The DRA government, like its army, was in transition. Dr Najibullah Ahmadzai succeeded President Babrak Karmal as the Afghan Communist Party secretary in May 1986. Desertion was a major problem and a new conscription system was introduced, making access to higher education dependent on completion of military service, which was compulsory for all eighteen-year-olds.

The first US Stinger anti-aircraft missiles reached the Mujahideen in April 1986 and the Afghan Army made an even greater effort to cut the rebels' supply route across the Pakistani border. In fact the Afghan Army assumed the burden of the fighting when elements of five divisions, up to 15,000 men, supported by around 2,000 Soviets, launched a major attack in Paktia province once again. By now 70 per cent of Soviet operations were heliborne, leaving the Afghan Army to do the ground fighting. Soviet Special Forces, a combination of Spetsnaz and airborne troops, about 1,000 strong, formed one arm of a pincer movement designed to trap the Mujahideen at Zhawar.

In the spring 2,000 vehicles moved out of Khost on a sweep operation. Afghan troops unsuccessfully attacked Jaji Mayadan to the north-east of Khost and Tani to the south-west on 22 April 1986. They did, however, manage to capture the important Zhawar bunker complex near the border, claiming to have killed numerous guerrillas and captured large quantities of rebel weapon stocks.

Brigadier Yousaf observed:

> According to their account we had lost 2,000 dead and 4,000 wounded. To say that this propaganda stretched the truth would be a serious understatement. Mujahideen losses at Zhawar did not exceed 300 killed, together with a few truckloads of arms and ammunition. Although Zhawar base fell, other nearby strongpoints did not.

Although almost self-sufficient before the Soviet invasion, by 1988 Kabul was forced to import half a million tonnes of wheat annually from the Soviet Union, together with such staples as sugar, rice and oil to feed the population. By 1989 the Afghan government was only able to produce 10 per cent of what it required, some 150,000 tonnes, due to a bad harvest and the war. Resupply from across the Soviet border became vital, as did keeping the supply routes open.

This became a common sight on Afghanistan's roads – an ambushed convoy. Having killed or driven off the drivers and their guards, these Mujahideen have come down from the hills for a closer look at their handiwork. (*IAAM*)

The Mujahideen excelled in this terrain and the geography greatly favoured them. These men are at the Tari observation post just before launching a mortar attack on the Shigal Tarna garrison in Kunar province. Note the man on the left has an RPG slung over his shoulder. (*Erwin Franzen*)

Afghans watch a supply column snaking along below them. The 500-mile road from the Soviet frontier down to Kabul was a vital lifeline to the Soviet and Afghan Armies – as a result it was constantly attacked. (*Via Author*)

This Soviet BTR armoured personnel carrier was photographed outside Bagram air base – the latter provided another vital link with the Soviet Union and was something the guerrillas regularly attempted to sever by attacking the garrison and rocketing the runway. (*Via Author*)

Mujahideen examine a bullet-riddled jeep following a successful ambush. Due to Soviet air supremacy the resistance made very little use of vehicles other than to ferry supplies over the Pakistani border. (*AIO/Julian Gearing*)

The victims of a successful guerrilla attack on a convoy near Asmar in 1985. The damaged gun is a Soviet D-30 122mm field gun. In the background are the burnt-out cabs of various lorries. (*Erwin Franzen*)

A resistance fighter armed with a RPG-7 grenade launcher heads home to Badakshan, Nuristan province in 1985. He is clearly ready for action as his RPG is loaded. The pack animal is probably carrying vital supplies for his group. (*AIO/Julian Gearing*)

This pack horse ferries mines to the resistance at the dead of night. These plastic anti-tank mines were standard guerrilla weapons. Although not actually produced in Italy, Soviet troops knew then as the 'Italian mine'. The Mujahideen ended up with so many mines they took to removing the explosives to use to fuel their stoves. These smugglers were photographed in Paktia in 1984. (*Erwin Franzen*)

This time a camel is used by the Mujahideen to carry weaponry over the mountains between Afghanistan and Pakistan. (*Erwin Franzen*)

Jaji, Pakti province in August 1984. An Afghan trader and his camels make their way to the lowlands over the border in Pakistan, passing a Mujahid on his way to fight the *shuravi* (the Soviets and their allies). (*Erwin Franzen*)

Sayyaf group Mujahideen camping in Jaji in August 1984. They are probably gun running. Using vehicles too far from the border tended to attract the attentions of the Soviet Air Force. (*Erwin Franzen*)

A Soviet engineer tank, based on the T-55, being used to clear debris from a road following an ambush; the tank on the roadside appears to have struck a mine. (*Igor Bondarets*)

More evidence of a successful resistance attack on an exposed stretch of highway. The destroyed tankers have been shunted off the road and left to rust on the banks of a nearby river. (*Igor Bondarets*)

This Soviet soldier seated on a BTR turret takes a break from unrelenting convoy duties.
(*Igor Bondarets*)

More Soviet troops on convoy duty pose for the camera – the vehicle in the background appears to be a BMP-2. The man on the left is holding a PKM 7.62mm medium machine gun.
(*Igor Bondarets*)

Two apprehensive-looking Soviet prisoners face an uncertain future at the hands of their Mujahideen captors. (*Via Author*)

Time for a swim? The crew of a BTR take time out from the war for some frivolity and R&R. (*Igor Bondarets*)

Mujahideen travelling by foot and horse heading north in Jaji, Paktia in 1984. (*Erwin Franzen*)

A Mujahid shows off his heavy machine gun, which appears to have been taken from a Soviet tank. (*IAAM*)

The Chinese Type 56 assault rifle (the fixed-stock variant was fitted with a folding bayonet) provided the backbone of the guerrillas' small arms. Below it is a captured Soviet 80mm RPG-22 disposable anti-tank rocket launcher. (*Author's Collection*)

This Soviet truck has driven over a land mine that blew the front right-hand-side wheel clean off. Luckily on this occasion no one seems to have been harmed. The men in the foreground are armed with the AK-74 assault rifle and are presumably waiting for a recovery vehicle. (*Igor Bondarets*)

This column of Soviet BTR APCs has stopped for a break on a particularly vulnerable stretch of road. The steep sides of the gorge illustrate the type of conditions that were ideal for an ambush. (*Igor Bondarets*)

Chapter Seven

Death over the Mountains

The primary Soviet weapon in Afghanistan was undoubtedly the helicopter. In particular the Gorbach (or Hunchback) Mil Mi-24 Hind helicopter gunship was instrumental and the weapon most feared by the guerrillas. In 1982 the Soviets deployed up to 600 helicopters to Afghanistan, of which 200 were Mi-24s. They were used rather than fixed-wing aircraft for most of the CAS missions, adopting nap-of-the-earth tactics, especially once the Mujahideen's air defences became more sophisticated.

In addition it was the Soviet Sukhoi Su-25 Frogfoot ground attack aircraft that also proved to be most effective, with a high survivability against SA-7 SAMs. In April 1986 during the Zhawar campaign Su-25s used laser-guided bombs to hit Mujahideen caves with great accuracy.

Prior to the Soviet intervention the Afghan Air Force (AAF) had about 169 combat aircraft. With the rural revolt in Afghanistan spreading, the Soviet Union increased deliveries to Bagram, including Mi-24s, MiGs and Sus. They demonstrated their faith in air power over the insurgency by supplying the AAF with six MiG-21 Fishbed fighters, twelve Mi-24 Hind helicopter gunships, as well as a number of Su-20 Fitter fighter bombers and Mi-6 Hook medium/heavy-lift helicopters. This was the first occasion that the AAF received the Mi-24 and Su-20; it also required an increase in Soviet advisers from 1,000 to 5,000, thereby making the AAF even more reliant on Moscow.

After the Soviet intervention, the AAF, consisting of about seven fighter, helicopter and transport regiments, was co-located with Soviet units – largely to avoid defection. Between 1979 and 1988 there were at least six defections by Afghan pilots to Pakistan with MiG-19, MiG-21 and Mi-24 aircraft.

The Soviet Air Force (Vozduyushno Voorezhenie Sil – VVS, consisting of the Strategic Air Armies, Air Force of the Military Districts and Groups of Forces and Military Transport Aviation, VTA) by June 1980 had begun to play a far greater role in supporting the ground war in Afghanistan. One operation reportedly involved sixteen helicopters, practically a whole regiment, against just one village, at a stage when the total number deployed VVS helicopters only numbered around fifty.

The LCSFA began to reorganise in June 1980 in order to meet the growing requirements of a wider counter-insurgency war. This resulted in the VVS deploying new units, with a large increase in the number of helicopters, rising from fifty to 300 by the following year. Three whole helicopter regiments were deployed to Bagram, Konduz and Kandahar as well as a number of supporting independent units.

By the end of 1980 there were about 130 Soviet fighter aircraft, mainly MiG-21s, Su-17s and MiG-23s flying from Bagram, Shindand and Herat. The regimental HQ, though, remained in the Turkestan and central Asian military districts, enabling better control and maintenance.

The ground-striking arm of the Soviet helicopter force was provided by five air assault brigades. Most of the troop-carrying and resupply missions were conducted by the Mi-8 Hip (also capable of an attack role) supported by the larger Mi-6 Hook. By 1983 the Soviets had deployed 150 Mi-8s and forty Mi-6s.

The number of helicopters serving in Afghanistan had fallen to 350 by 1985. Also that year the Soviets reportedly tested the Mi-28 Havoc attack/anti-tank helicopter in Afghanistan. The Soviets fielded 275 helicopters in February 1988, and the AAF about eighty, organised into two regiments.

The growing reliance on helicopters did impose operational limitations. Engines overheated, were less efficient at high altitude and there were problems with ice during the winter. Environmentally this restricted efficient operations to the spring or autumn. Also the Mujahideen claimed that the guns and rockets on the Mi-24 did not have a high kill ratio, though they were difficult to shoot down, which gave them a greater combat linger time.

The VVS based in Afghanistan was on a rotational basis, allowing most of the maintenance to be carried out in the Soviet Union. The main parent units were the 27th Fighter Aviation Regiment at Kaka and the 217th Fighter Bomber Regiment at Kirzyl Arvat. In 1985 there were ten squadrons with 12–15 aircraft each in Afghanistan with the same number in the Soviet Union flying support missions. There were two or three squadrons of MiG-23s and MiG-27 Floggers, one or two squadrons of MiG-21 Fishbeds and two squadrons each of Su-17 Fitters and Su-25 Frogfoots. By 1984 the MiG-21 had been replaced by the MiG-23 and MiG-27.

Retard, RBK-250 cluster, laser-guided and even 12,000lb bombs were introduced, as well as high-altitude bombing. An example of this occurred in April 1984 when thirty-six Tu-16 Badger bombers were concentrated in the Turkestan military district for high-level bombing of the Panjsher valley in support of the Soviets' seventh offensive there. The newer T-26 Backfire was first deployed into Afghanistan in November 1988. VTA An-12 Cubs and An-26 Curls were used for reconnaissance and master bomber roles. The older Soviet Il-28 Beagle bomber was deployed by the AAF's 355th Air Regiment at Shindand.

Between 1980 and 1983 several dozen helicopters were lost, to multiple causes, but an increasing use of flares by 1983 showed a growing fear of infra-red heat-seeking missiles. Mujahideen in Kandahar reportedly using an American Stinger shot down a Bakhtar Airlines Antonov on 3 September 1985. The following year the Soviets were becoming increasingly alarmed by the Mujahideen's use of SAMs, with aircraft routinely employing flares on takeoff and landing.

In March 1986 it was made clear the US had decided to supply the Stinger to the Mujahideen, based on the Soviets' growing reliance on helicopters and the guerrillas' inability to counter them effectively. An initial batch of 200 was delivered in October 1986; by the time the US ceased supplying them at the start of 1989 the Mujahideen had received about 1,000 missiles.

The first effective use of a Stinger was reported in the eastern province of Nangarhar. In the Zhawar campaign in 1986 the Soviets lost twelve helicopters and one fighter. During the first two weeks of November eleven helicopters and one MiG-23 were reported shot down. By the end of 1986 the Soviets had lost a total of 500 helicopters to all causes, and by 1988 it was claimed Stinger alone had shot down 100 Soviet/Afghan aircraft of all types.

Stingers also closed the airfield at Khost, which sparked off the Soviets' last major offensive of the war in December 1987 – in which heliborne forces played a prominent role. Despite the US cutting off weapon supplies in February 1989, Soviet and Afghan bombers continued to fly at high altitude for fear of Stingers.

The Soviets were accused of conducting a scorched-earth policy using aircraft and artillery in January 1989 to cover their final withdrawal operations. Certainly a slackening of the Mujahideen's SAM defences at Kandahar may have prompted the VVS and AAF to intensify their attacks. AAF MiG-21s armed with cluster bombs defending Jalalabad in some cases attacked at low altitude, improving accuracy. In the first two weeks of February the Soviet Air Force conducted 350 sorties over Afghanistan as the final pullout took place.

A view that filled the Mujahideen with fear – until the delivery of the American Stinger missile the resistance found it almost impossible to counter the heavy firepower (which included missiles, rockets and bombs) of the Hind. (*US DoD*)

The most significant weapon in the Soviet–Afghan War was undoubtedly the Mi-24 Hind-D. In 1982 the Soviets deployed up to 600 helicopters to Afghanistan, of which a third were Mi-24s. (*Author's Collection*)

The Soviets ensured their transport helicopters also had an air assault role. The highly successful Mi-8/17 Hip appeared in the 1960s, providing a cheap alternative to gunship or attack helicopters, and was exported around the world, seeing action in countless wars. (*Author's Collection*)

The Sukhoi Su-25 Frogfoot close-support aircraft first deployed to Afghanistan in 1981, initially operating from Bagram and then Shindand. A second squadron was stationed at Bagram by early 1986. It was the Su-25's high survivability against the Soviet SA-7 Grail SAM used by the resistance that convinced America to supply the Stinger to the Mujahideen. (*US DoD*)

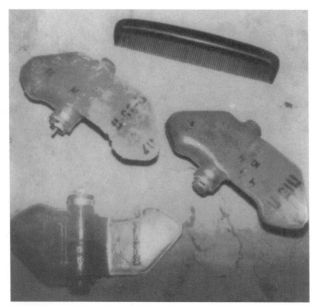

The tiny PFM-1 Butterfly mine was dropped in large numbers right across Afghanistan. They could lie dormant for up to six months before self-detonating – however, picking it up would cause it to explode immediately. Children were particularly vulnerable to this insidious weapon. (*AIO/Julian Gearing*)

A Soviet Hind-D unleashes its Swatter anti-tank guided missiles (ATGM) at an unsuspecting target; visible are some of its four 57mm rocket pods, launch rails for the ATGMs and 12.7mm Gatling gun with radar and sensors under the nose. (*US DoD*)

Caught in the act by a resistance photographer, this time a Hip-E attack helicopter attempts to knock out Mujahideen positions. It is identifiable by the struts supporting the short wings with the weapon pylons. Such attacks were often made while under fire. Even transport Hips were armed, but by 1984 only the Hinds tended to conduct attack missions due to increasing resistance air defence. (*Author's Collection*)

A serious-faced Soviet helicopter pilot – initially he and his comrades had free rein over Afghanistan, but slowly losses mounted as the guerrillas developed increasingly effective countermeasures. (*Via Author*)

A Soviet gunner engages ground targets; the Hip acted as a very effective attack helicopter in support of the Hinds. (*Via Author*)

A blurred resistance shot of an M-24 Hind going in for the kill in Afghanistan. Shortly after the Soviet invasion rebels shot one down for the very first time using the SA-7 SAM. Of the 1,000 aircraft lost by 1987 over 80 per cent were helicopters, of which a third were Hinds. (*Author's Collection*)

The 'Dashika' 12.7mm DShKM heavy machine gun (both Soviet- and Chinese-built versions) was the standard Mujahideen air defence weapon. Most guerrilla strongholds were protected by several such machine-gun positions. This gunner was photographed in Jaji, Paktia in the summer of 1984. (*Erwin Franzen*)

These fighters are preparing Chinese-made 107mm rockets for an attack on Barikot in Kunar province in August 1985. The guerrillas also used rockets against enemy aircraft with mixed results. Growing availability of these weapons gave the resistance a greater stand-off fighting capability. (*Erwin Franzen*)

Resistance fighters from the Jamiat-i-Islami group in the Shultan valley, Kunar with their 'Dashika' in October 1987. These guns were often positioned high up so they could shoot down onto passing helicopters. (*Erwin Franzen*)

Dud bombs became a familiar sight in Afghanistan. Journalist Erwin Franzen examines the debris in Jaji, Paktia province in August 1984. (*Erwin Franzen*)

Another large Soviet bomb canister photographed in an orchard in Jaji, in 1984. The fruit tree narrowly avoided being blown to oblivion. Jettisoned fuel tanks were also sometimes mistaken for unexploded munitions. (*Erwin Franzen*)

Yunus Khalis
Mujahideen in the
Shultan valley north
of Asadabad in Kunar
province in October
1987. This bomb has
also buried itself
head-first and failed
to go off. (*Erwin
Franzen*)

This unexploded munitions seems to have buried itself tail-first in Jaji in 1984. (*Erwin Franzen*)

Every helicopter combat pilot's greatest fear: this Afghan Army Mi-4 Hound helicopter was shot down by the resistance in March 1979 in Nuristan province just before the Soviet invasion. (*US DoD*)

This Mi-8 Hip seems to have crash-landed; note the rocket pod on the ground to the right having snapped off its pylon. The one on the left remains attached. By 1988 over 1,000 Soviet and Afghan aircraft had been lost, though half the helicopter losses were due to operational accidents rather than enemy action. (*Igor Bondarets*)

This fighter poses with the weapon credited with driving the Soviets from Afghanistan – the General Dynamics heat-seeking Stinger SAM. The Mujahideen soon learned how to get the most out of this weapon. (*Via Author*)

The Tupolev Tu-16 Badger multi-role bomber was used to conduct high-level bombing, including that of Ahmad Shah Massoud's stronghold in the Panjsher valley. The guerrillas had no answer to such attacks and could only take shelter in their mountain caves and hope for the best. (*US DoD*)

The newer T-26 Backfire was first deployed into Afghanistan in November 1988; these were capable of launching stand-off cruise missiles as well as guided bombs. (*Author's Collection*)

The ancient Tu-95 Bear strategic bomber may have conducted high-level bombing attacks in Afghanistan. Its range and operating altitude would have meant it could operate with impunity. (*Author's Collection*)

Another very grainy resistance photo – having brought down a Soviet Hip transport helicopter these resistance fighters give thanks to Allah. (*Via Author*)

Afghan villagers come to have a look at a very large unexploded Soviet bomb. The resistance became very adept at defusing such UXBs and removing the explosives for subsequent use in mines. Nonetheless they posed a severe danger to civilians. (*IAAM*)

An Afghan village thought to be harbouring resistance fighters is shrouded in a pall of smoke following a missile and rocket attack by a Mi-24 Hind helicopter gunship. (*Author's Collection*)

A close-up of a rocket pod from a crashed Mi-24 gunship. The guerrillas often recovered the explosives from such ordnance and reused them in their own home-made bombs and mines. (*IAAM*)

Chapter Eight

Moscow's Last Stand

Operation Magistral was the last major offensive conducted by the Soviet Union during its ill-fated intervention in Afghanistan. The battle for Khost, initiated to lift the siege and cut the Mujahideen's supply routes once and for all, was probably the bloodiest of the war. Orchestrated by the Soviets to prove the Afghan Army's fighting capabilities, it involved 24,000 Afghan and Soviet troops sent to rescue the 8,000-strong garrison that was trapped by up to 20,000 Mujahideen.

By October 1987 the Mujahideen, with the help of US-supplied Stinger surface-to-air missiles, had tightened their siege of Khost, its air links had been cut and the town was under severe threat. Khost had been under close siege for three months, though its land links had been continually disrupted for seven long years. The inhabitants, including army personnel, were faced with growing shortages, and the civilian population of about 40,000 had begun to flee. Between November and December 1987 food prices soared, with the cost of wheat and rice doubling. The trapped garrison consisted of the 25th Afghan Infantry Division and the Frontier Guard's 2nd Brigade along with several hundred Soviet advisers.

Brigadier Mohammad Yousaf, head of the Pakistani Inter-Service Intelligence's Afghan Bureau, recalled in his memoirs:

> Khost was surrounded by mountains in which sat the Mujahideen. All around were a series of defensive posts and minefields, with a substantial garrison at Tani. The Mujahideen were particularly strong to the south and SE of the town, with their outposts overlooking the plain . . . the totally exposed airfield . . . was seldom used by the Afghans as we could bring it under fire so easily that they often resorted to parachute dropping of supplies.

The rising Soviet death toll in Afghanistan and public opinion back home finally began affecting Soviet policy. President Mikhail Gorbachev announced in mid-1986 a limited withdrawal as a sign of goodwill in the ongoing peace negotiations. This move naturally concerned Afghan President Najibullah and was met with scepticism by the West. This view was reinforced in October 1986 when units with no tactical value were the ones pulled out. Nonetheless, Gorbachev made it clear that he wanted to leave Afghanistan.

On 15 January 1987 Gorbachev and Najibullah renewed their peace initiatives by holding a unilateral ceasefire. Najibullah supported a complete Soviet withdrawal after the acceptance of the ceasefire by the rebels. Two days later talks were held in Pakistan between Soviet and US representatives. Pakistan advocated a withdrawal within a matter of months, to ensure the Soviets would not have time to crush the Mujahideen, who technically under the proposed Western agreement would lose US military aid. However, any settlement had to satisfy Kabul, Moscow, Washington, the Mujahideen, Islamabad and Tehran, making consensus almost impossible.

The Afghan government decided in the face of an imminent Soviet withdrawal that it must at all costs avoid the loss of Khost and sever the rebels' supply routes. Ostensibly an Afghan operation, the relief was commanded by Major-General Shahnawaz Tani (although he was to be subordinate to the Soviets) and Major-General Mohammed Gulabzoi, the interior minister. On the Soviet side General Valentin Varennikov, senior military adviser to Kabul, oversaw the operation, with operational control in the hands of Lieutenant-General Boris Gromov, commander of the Soviet 40th Army.

The government amassed 24,000 Afghan/Soviet troops and the relief effort represented the last major combined operation. The Afghan III Corps HQ at Gardez organised five divisions backed by two Soviet divisions (consisting of roughly 10,000 paratroops from the 103rd Guards Air Assault Division and the 38th Air Assault Brigade, plus some 6,000 men from a motor rifle division), with 650 supply trucks protected by seventy jet fighters. Against this impressive attacking force the Mujahideen were to put up a stiff fight.

The drive on Khost was channelled down 122km of guerrilla-infested road, through the Satu Kandau pass and down the Zadran valley. The Mujahideen, although lacking heavy weapons, had plenty of RPGs to make the passage of the relief force highly dangerous. The outlying Afghan Army posts in the area were awkward to defend (consisting of Tora Ghara mountain, Badam Bagh, Khost air base, Sinaki and fort Nadar Shah Kot), all of which were directed by just forty-three Soviet advisers.

Initially only employing Afghan troops, the offensive was launched on 18 November 1987 and it immediately ran into tough resistance in the Shamal valley off Zadran and elsewhere along the route. With the Soviets providing air support, on 24 November they captured positions in Ghalgai, Dara, Makhuzu, Sarooti Kandau and Shini Ghakhe. The Soviet airborne forces also took three important mountain passes at Sarooti Kandau, Khadi Kandau and Satu Kandau on the 28th.

A month later, on 28 December, the Soviets claimed to be within 9km of Khost, while the guerrillas claimed to have halted them 48km away. That day a further attack on Saranai failed and Soviet paratroops lost sixty-three men as they withdrew, hotly pursued by the vengeful Mujahideen. The Khost garrison again attempted to break out, reaching Ismail Khel 10 km to the west before being driven back once more.

Khost was finally relieved on 30 December when trucks bearing 4,500 tonnes of supplies rumbled into the town. The Soviet paratroops launched a mopping-up operation on 2 January 1988 when 7,000 men were deployed 60km to the north to trap the withdrawing Mujahideen; a further 1,500 were deployed in the surrounding hills. By 20 January 400 supply trucks had got through, bringing 18,000 tonnes of much-needed provisions. Ironically, as soon as the Afghan/Soviet forces withdrew from Khost the Mujahideen simply resumed their blockade.

The drive on Khost cost the Afghan and Soviet Armies dearly. Between 18 and 29 December 1987, according to the Mujahideen, the Afghan Army lost 1,000 dead, possibly 2,000 wounded and 346 PoWs. About 110 AFVs were destroyed, including forty-seven tanks, as well as seven aircraft. The Soviets suffered very heavy casualties by normal standards, with at least 320 killed and some 600 wounded. Reports of Mujahideen casualties ranged from 150 to 1,500, with possibly 2,000 wounded. Some 60,000 civilians fled from the Zadran valley into Pakistan as a result of the fighting.

Moscow still had approximately 115,000 troops in Afghanistan, with another 40,000 stationed just over the border, as well as 50,000 support troops. By June 1988 the Soviet intervention had cost Moscow a total of 13,310 dead, 33,478 wounded and 311 missing. Afghan government losses are estimated at 20,000, and Mujahideen/civilian up to a million.

Moscow announced on 11 January 1988 it was prepared to commence with-drawing by 1 May contingent on an Afghan–Pakistani agreement. This date was pushed back when Gorbachev announced that Soviet troops would begin withdrawing on 15 May 1988 to coincide with the next Superpower summit, and would be completed by 15 February 1989. This finally brought an end to the decade-long Soviet–Afghan War. It did not bring a close to the bitter fighting.

Although officially an Afghan government offensive, Soviet General Valentin Varennikov oversaw Operation Magistral in late 1987 from the safety of Kabul, while General Boris Gromov exercised operational control. (*Author's Collection*)

General Boris Gromov had the unenviable task of extricating the Soviet armed forces from Afghanistan with the minimum of casualties. His view was that the Soviet–Afghan War was 'an irreparable political mistake by the Soviet leadership'. (*Author's Collection*)

Soviet infantry on their BMP-2s getting ready to jump off on an operation. In late 1987 the Soviets and their Afghan allies sought to drive the Mujahideen away from Khost and the Afghan–Pakistan border as a prelude to Moscow's withdrawal. (*Igor Bondarets*)

Soviet Spetsnaz (Spetsialnoye Naznachenie) preparing for a mission. These men specialised in dropping in behind enemy lines and could expect little mercy if captured. (*Via Author*)

Mi-8 Hip disgorging troops in a heliborne assault. Moscow became far too reliant on helicopters during the Soviet–Afghan War. (*Via Author*)

This camouflaged 12.7mm heavy machine gun is typical of the positions that the Soviets had to fight their way through during Operation Magistral. (*Erwin Franzen*)

The fearsome-looking Soviet DShKM 12.7mm heavy machine gun is redeployed against its former owners. This weapon was used against soft-skinned vehicles as well as helicopters. (*AIO/Julian Gearing*)

Very confident-looking guerrillas proudly brandishing their Kalashnikovs. (*IAAM/Jonas Dovydenas*)

A Soviet column pushes forward under supporting fire. By the late 1980s the Mujahideen were not prepared to give ground. (*Igor Bondarets*)

This weapon is the versatile 82mm Vasilyek 2B9 automatic mortar that was extensively used in Afghanistan. It can be used in both direct and indirect fire modes. During the conflict some had their wheels removed and were fitted on the rear deck of the MT-LB tracked armoured vehicle. This is believed to have been a battlefield conversion. (*Igor Bondarets*)

These men look about ready to go home. Three of them have tanker helmets, which identifies them as armoured vehicle crew. They are carrying the AK-74S assault rifle. (*Igor Bondarets*)

Somewhere up in the Afghan mountains. Taking a break from the cramped interior of their BMP-2, again these men have a rather resigned look despite the half-hearted smile from their driver. Although public opinion did not sway Moscow after ten years of involvement in Afghanistan the Soviet Union had war fatigue. (*Igor Bondarets*)

Soviet Spetsnaz Special Forces interrogate an elderly looking prisoner – they took a leading role in Operation Magistral and helped prevent the armoured push to Khost from getting bogged down. (*E. Kuvakin*)

Having completed their mission unscathed, these BMP crewmen give each other a warm hug; as the date for the Soviet withdrawal drew ever closer the troops became understandably risk averse. (*Igor Bondarets*)

BMP-2s were employed by the 70th Motorised Rifle Brigade near Kandahar. The chassis is almost identical to the earlier BMP-1 but has increased armour protection and the commander occupies the turret instead of sitting behind the driver. The 30mm cannon proved highly effective in providing fire support for Soviet troops and it was a much better weapon than the BMP-1's 73mm gun. (*US DoD*)

An up-armoured T-62M of the 'Berlin' tank regiment, 5th Guards Motorised Rifle Division, leaving Afghanistan in 1987 as part of President Gorbachev's withdrawal announcement. (*US DoD*)

The pullout of Soviet troops from Afghanistan in 1988. An Afghan Army BTR-60PB is passing a halted column of Soviet BTR-80s. A BMP-1 or BMP-2 is just visible behind the Afghan vehicle. (*Mikhail Evstafiev*)

T-72 tank crew preparing to go home. (*Author's Collection*)

An air assault forces' BMD on patrol in Kabul; this vehicle proved to be quite effective – in contrast the ASU-85 was rapidly withdrawn from service as its hull gun was not suited for counter-insurgency warfare. (*US DoD*)

This was how the West saw the Soviet Union's humiliation in Afghanistan. The country had become a deadly trap for the Russian bear. (*IAAM*)

Chapter Nine

Propping up Kabul

It was widely expected that President Najibullah's regime would rapidly collapse after the Soviet withdrawal on 15 February 1989. In reality two key factors brought this assessment into question: the morale of the Afghan Army – would it fight on alone – and would the government be able to materially sustain itself?

Ultimately the Soviet Union ensured both challenges were met as a land and air bridge kept Kabul well supplied with food and guns both before and after the Soviet pullout. Convoys of up to 2,000 vehicles pushed across the border and an increasing number of flights flew into the Afghan capital. Sustained by this massive aid Moscow underwrote Najibullah and the Afghan Army was able confidently to face down the advancing Mujahideen.

The Soviet land bridge, despite constant attacks, provided Kabul with a large stockpile of weapons and ammunition. This was illustrated by the Mujahideen attack before the withdrawal on the Soviet garrison at Kilagay, in Baghlan province north of the capital. The raid took place on 10/11 August 1988 and the camp reportedly contained most of the Afghan government's ammunition stocks, enough for two years, as well as substantial fuel reserves. All this was blown up and a pro-government militia source claimed 598 Soviet soldiers and 112 civilians were killed, with a further 284 wounded in the massive blasts.

The guerrillas were only too well aware of the importance of these stockpiles as the Soviet retreat began to gather pace. A Mujahideen rocket attack on Kabul airport on 9 September 1988 hit a transport aircraft loaded with ammunition and weapons. Another lucky strike hit the airport's main ammunition depot, triggering a series of explosions that lasted several hours.

In the run-up to the pullout a whole series of battles were fought to keep the vital Salang tunnel and highway north of the capital open. By early February 1989 local reports indicated heavy fighting in and around Charikar. General M.A. Delawar, Afghan Chief of the General Staff, denied suggestions that the fighting had stranded a 200-vehicle convoy just to the north. Even so, a Soviet officer confirmed that the Afghan Army was deploying newly acquired BM-27 multiple-rocket launchers, given to the Special Guard, north of Kabul to clear a route to the Soviet border.

To the south-east, at the end of January 1989 the Mujahideen, in order to avoid giving the impression of starving their own people, allowed forty-three trucks of flour and other supplies into the city of Jalalabad, giving it a much-needed breathing space. When the Soviet forces finally departed it was left to the Afghan Army to maintain the land bridge on its own.

On 4/5 March 1989 a convoy of 556 vehicles with 6,000 tonnes of food got through to the capital. This, though, was after a deal had been struck with the Kabul province and Salang area Mujahideen commander. Despite this the guerrillas attacked a convoy of lorries north of Kabul on 5 March, setting fire to fifteen vehicles carrying fuel and other supplies. The Mujahideen reportedly used SAMs to destroy thirteen oil tankers and two other trucks in the Karabagh-Kerezmir area of Kabul province.

During April 1989 another convoy of about 700 vehicles struggled to get through to Kabul. On 14 April, ninety trucks reached the capital, but two days later at least 200 were stranded on the Salang highway with twenty hit by the guerrillas. This continued blockade caused a pile-up of about 140,000 tonnes of vital food along the Soviet border.

In a show of strength the Afghan Army pushed an armoured column of over 600 vehicles, including 200 tanks, into Kabul on 25 May 1989. The T-54 and T-62 tanks were virtually the backbone of an armoured division, and had previously been used along American lines as mobile firebases in the defence of Afghanistan's cities. The column also included a regiment of artillery and tractors piled with ammunition.

To the south, after the airport at Kandahar became unsafe, a convoy of 1,000 vehicles took over a month to reach the city from the Soviet border, arriving towards the end of September 1989. Initially it was held up 48km outside Kandahar, losing eighty vehicles in one attack.

Kabul's most experienced convoy trouble-shooter was Deputy Prime Minister General Mohammed Hakim, who had organised the relief convoy to Khost in 1987 and saved Kabul from starvation in 1988. He claimed by the beginning of October 1989, 'We are receiving 300 trucks of supplies a day from the Soviet Union.' At the beginning of November 2,000 trucks passed through the Salang tunnel to Kabul. This support helped keep Kabul fed and armed throughout the winter.

Probably of greater importance and easier to maintain was the Soviet air bridge. It was a relatively safe and efficient way of ferrying arms to the Afghan Army. By the end of March 1988 the Soviet Union was flying arms into Kabul at an ever-increasing rate. By the first week in April 1988 aircraft were landing and taking off at Kabul every one or two hours, the volume possibly indicating the resupply of additional areas outside the capital.

Observers in Kabul spotted an An-12 transport aircraft with government markings for the first time on 23 May, indicating that they had probably been resupplied after the 15 May arms embargo. Until then the An-12s were only used by the Soviets in Afghanistan: the VTA had deployed about 125 of them.

Before the final Soviet pullout and in line with their pledge to keep Kabul armed, Moscow sent large quantities of arms and ammunition during January 1989. These shipments included BTR-70 APCs and BM-27s. Ilyushin-76 transport flights in and out of the capital were running at seven a day. The Afghan Army also took delivery of a number of FROG-7 rocket launchers. These were supplied with life-expired FROG-7a/b rockets from Soviet stocks and replaced the 1,000 or so Scud-B missiles that had been provided previously.

During the winter of 1989 it was thought the Soviet air bridge would not be able to sustain Kabul, which needed 60 tonnes of flour and 1,200 tonnes of fuel a day. In fact the volume of Soviet flights increased dramatically. The crisis emerging from the Mujahideen's blockade of the land bridge was averted as the Soviets airlifted in 3,500 tonnes of flour and other supplies.

Soviet aircraft also flew 350 combat missions over Afghanistan, covering broad areas of the countryside with bombs during the two weeks before the completion of the withdrawal. Having averted starvation, in mid-March 1989 over sixty Il-76s flew into Kabul, resuming Soviet arms shipments, which had reportedly halted after the withdrawal. Soviet aid was estimated to be worth up to $300 million a month with forty flights a day bringing in ammunition and FROG-7 rockets.

This massive Soviet logistical support to the Afghan government not only provided bread and weapons with which to defend itself, but also a psychological boost that helped Najibullah's regime hold on during the dangerous transition period. The Soviets' logistic system not only enabled Moscow to sustain a ten-year counter-insurgency war in Afghanistan, but also to prop up Najibullah successfully for a number of years after their withdrawal.

In the run-up to the Soviet withdrawal from Afghanistan, Moscow shipped ever-increasing quantities of military hardware to the Afghan Army in an effort to prop it up, including tanks and other armoured vehicle. (*US DoD*)

Lacking punch for convoy escort duties the BRDM-2 scout car was ideal for policing the city streets and a number were handed over to the Afghan police. (*US DoD*)

An Afghan Army BM-21 rocket launcher on the outskirts of Kabul. Moscow ensured that the Afghan government forces had plenty of these weapon systems as it enabled them to keep the Mujahideen at arm's length and away from the capital. (*US DoD*)

More Soviet-supplied Grad rocket launchers captured by the resistance. (*Via Author*)

Guerrillas inspecting Soviet rockets. Civilians suffered dreadfully as they were normally caught in the middle during indiscriminate rocket attacks. (*Erwin Franzen*)

Fighters on the Afghan–Pakistani border. Once the Soviet Army had gone the Afghan Army did not have the resources to control the border crossings. (*Erwin Franzen*)

A group of fighters pose for the camera – many of the Mujahideen factions hoped that the Soviet withdrawal would bring peace, but it was not to be. These men are under Commander Ajab Khan and are from the Yunus Khalis group. (*Erwin Franzen*)

More fighters in Kunar. (*Erwin Franzen*)

The resistance was even able to bring supplies in by helicopter once the Soviet Air Force was no longer a threat. These fighters are unloading rockets from an old Soviet Hip. (*Via Author*)

A heart-stopping moment. The RPG gunner on the right is aiming right for the cameraman, in this case journalist Erwin Franzen. The fighter at the back is holding an AK-47 assault rifle and an RPD light machine gun. (*Erwin Franzen*)

Another former Afghan Army BM-21 Grad rocket launchers. (*US DoD*)

More Yunus Khalis Mujahideen. Some of them are wearing chest pouches to hold spare magazines for their Kalashnikovs. (*Erwin Frazen*)

Afghan elders holding a *shura* or meeting to decide their next course of action; once the Soviets had pulled out, the Mujahideen attempted to capture Kabul and Kandahar with little success. Their attacks wilted in the face of the Afghan Army's superior firepower. (*Author's Collection*)

So much junk: the legacy of the Soviet–Afghan War and the subsequent civil war – rusting Soviet-built tanks. (*US DoD*)

The empty shell of the former royal Darulaman Palace in Kabul and one-time Soviet 40th Army HQ – it has come to symbolise the decades of destruction wrought on the country. (*Via Author*)

The face of victory. After the withdrawal of the Soviet Army in 1989 the Mujahideen were triumphant; however, the Communist-backed government in Kabul clung on for a number of years. Even when it did finally crumble it was not long before the various guerrilla factions fell out and the country was plunged into civil war. It was against this background that the Taliban came to power. (*IAAM*)

Chapter Ten

The Taliban's Tanks

The Soviet–Afghan War left a terrible legacy. Following the Soviets' departure Afghanistan soon descended into civil war as the various Mujahideen groups fell out and major weapon supplies ceased. It was several years before the guerrillas succeeded in capturing battered Kabul and then they resorted to taking up arms against each other. The former DRA and guerrilla forces lay in bloody disarray.

From this chaos emerged the Pakistani-backed Taliban, the successors to the Mujahideen, who seized power in the mid-1990s. The Taliban's decision to shelter Osama bin Laden and his al-Qaeda terror group opened the country to yet another round of blood letting.

The world watched in awe as US air power first chewed up the Taliban's air force, its air defences and then its armour during Operation Enduring Freedom in Afghanistan. Although America rapidly came to the decision, in the wake of 9/11, that it wanted the Taliban government and al-Qaeda terrorists defeated, it did not want to do it at the cost of thousands of US troops on the ground. The solution was to use Close Air Support (CAS) and Special Forces operating alongside the Taliban's nemesis, the Northern Alliance. The Special Forces, equipped with laser designators, would pinpoint enemy targets for US air strikes.

It would be fair to say that at the time of the American-led offensive the Taliban had about 300 tanks, mostly old Soviet-built T-55s and some T-62s, along with perhaps several hundred tracked BMP-1/2 APCs, 500 wheeled BTR APCs and some BRDM scout cars. Most of these were leftovers from the Soviet–Afghan War and few were roadworthy.

Taliban mobile rocket launchers included some Soviet BM-21s and BM-14s, whilst there were probably no more than a handful of mobile surface-to-surface missile launchers of the Scud and FROG-7a/b variety. The biggest threat to the US Air Force came from the Taliban's SA-13 mobile surface-to-air missiles. The serviceability of all these vehicles was fairly chronic and it is doubtful that even half were operational. Certainly the Taliban did not operate any sizeable armoured units

The American-led air war opened on 7 October 2001. As well as attacking the

Taliban's infrastructure, Coalition bombers also struck dispersal areas: for example, catching exposed Taliban armour running for the hills north-west of Herat army barracks; at their armoured vehicle depot outside Kandahar; and at Pol-e-Charkhi vehicle maintenance and storage facility. The fact that the Taliban failed to move almost 100 vehicles from the Kandahar depot before the air attacks indicates that most of them were just broken-down old scrap. Similarly the failure to disperse the 300-odd vehicles at Pol-e-Charkhi before the bombing shows that they were also already junk. At both locations air strikes flattened the vast vehicle storage sheds.

Initially the bombing did not greatly affect the Taliban's ability to wage war against the Northern Alliance, only its ability to resist Coalition air attack. Until the concentrated attacks on the Taliban's field forces, the degradation of the Taliban's communications was the greatest hindrance to their conduct of the civil war against the Northern Alliance. Crucially, by the end of October the air strikes began to shift away from high-profile urban targets towards Taliban frontline positions.

Twelve days after the air campaign opened, America began to secretly insert its CAS teams. The men of Tiger 01 were infiltrated into northern Afghanistan on 19 October 2001 by two MH-53J Pavelow helicopters of the 160th Special Operations Aviation Regiment. In the next few days, liaising with General Fahim's opposition forces, they were involved in efforts to capture Bagram. This they found defended by some fifty armoured vehicles, including tanks, APCs and ZSU-23-4 self-propelled anti-aircraft artillery (AAA).

Heavy strikes, including carpet-bombing, were conducted on 31 October against Taliban forces near Bagram. Six hours of air strikes called in by Tiger 01 obliterated everything. The following day the strategic Taliban garrison at Kala Ata, guarding the approaches to Taloqan, was also attacked. The raids lasted for over four hours; the blasts were so severe that windows were rumoured to have broken up to 20km away.

Attacks also continued in the Kandahar and Mazar-e-Sharif areas. Within a week of this intense bombing the Taliban crumbled first at Mazar-e-Sharif, then Kabul and Jalalabad – they were in headlong flight to their stronghold at Kandahar. Team Tiger 02 helped General Dostrum capture Mazar-e-Sharif on 9 November 2001, seizing the vital airfield and opening the supply route to Uzbekistan. The team called in strikes directing US Marine Corps F/A-18 fighters and AC-130 Spectre gunships to silence the deadly ZSU-23-4s and T-55s, accounting for at least fifty vehicles.

In just a few days during early November the Taliban lost control of much of the country in the face of the Northern Alliance's rapid ground offensive. Also in the prelude to the Northern Alliance's advance, their old enemies the Russians shipped in several hundred tanks and APCs. The dramatic collapse of the Taliban army was due to a combination of American air attacks, defections and an unprecedented level of co-operation between rival anti-Taliban factions. The Northern Alliance quickly gained control of most of the cities north of a line extending from Herat in the west to Kabul in the east.

During the attack on Kabul on 11 November 2001, Tiger 01 team accounted for twenty-nine tanks plus numerous vehicles and artillery pieces. Three days later it was all over: Kabul had fallen to the Northern Alliance. Tiger 03, directed to help capture the city of Kunduz, destroyed fifty tanks, APCs, AAA and artillery. Texas 11 helped General Daoud's forces liberate Taloqan, the Northern Alliance's former HQ, and capture Kunduz. On 17 November they called in air strikes which claimed five tanks, nine BRDM, one BTR-70 and four trucks. Between 14 and 29 November their battle damage assessment included twelve Taliban tanks, five ZPU/ZSUs, three BMP/BM-21s, three BTR-70/BRDMs and fifty-one lorries. Texas 12, assigned to Hamid Karzi, Afghanistan's future president, at the town of Tarin Kowt, north of Kandahar, stopped a Taliban counter-attack involving over eighty vehicles including BRDM; 35–45 of them were destroyed.

Within just three months of the air campaign commencing, the Taliban government was routed. The Taliban troops trapped in Kunduz surrendered, abandoning up to 5,000 foreign supporters to flee or capitulate. After the fall of Kabul the Taliban retired to prepared positions in and around Kandahar, their spiritual heartland. By the end of November with the collapse of the Taliban field forces, the focus of the air campaign switched to the Kandahar area and Tora Bora near Jalalabad in eastern Afghanistan.

Kandahar surrendered to opposition forces on 7 December 2001, without a fight. The al-Qaeda fighters, trapped by the peaks and valleys of the 4,700m White Mountains, had lost most of their heavy equipment. They had nothing with which to shoot back at the opposition forces' exposed tanks perched on the foothills.

The opposition forces proceeded to pound the mountains with artillery, mortars, rockets and Russian-supplied T-62 tanks. In the clear blue skies American B-52s disgorged their heavy munitions in a continuing effort to smash the caves. To the defenders of Tora Bora it must have seemed as if the American and opposition forces were trying to pulverise the very rock itself. The main ground offensive started late on 13 December. The enemy scattered and it was quickly all over, bar the shouting.

This victory paved the way for another decade of warfare in Afghanistan in which NATO forces were pitted against the Taliban. To many it was a pointless repeat of the Soviet–Afghan War.

Despite the ending of the Soviet–Afghan War in 1989, the Soviet legacy never went away: Taliban fighters inspecting a T-62 tank and a BRMD-2 scout car, formerly of the Afghan Army – leftovers from the bitter conflict. (*Via Author*)

Taliban riding on a BMP infantry fighting vehicle. They have turned it against the ineffectual Mujahideen coalition attempting to rule after the Communist Afghan government fell in the early 1990s. (*Via Author*)

One of the few SA-13 SAMs, mounted on the MT-LB chassis, operated by the Taliban. This was considered a threat to Coalition air strikes in November 2001. (*Via Author*)

Two FROG-7 short-range battlefield rockets overrun by the Northern Alliance in late 2001. After the Soviet withdrawal the Afghan Army took delivery of a number of FROG-7 launchers. These were supplied with life-expired FROG-7a/b rounds from Soviet stocks and replaced the 1,000 or so Scud-B missiles that had been provided previously. (*Via Author*)

An ancient Soviet-supplied BM-14 rocket launcher. (*Via Author*)

Northern Alliance T-55 tanks engaging enemy targets during the push south on Kabul in December 2001. Ironically many of these were supplied by Russia, which was also keen to see the back of the Taliban. (*Via Author*)

A Taliban T-55 tank depot; most vehicles were remnants of the Soviet–Afghan War and were completely unserviceable. (*Via Author*)

A captured Taliban T-55 gets the once over. (*Via Author*)

A Northern Alliance T-55 triumphantly entering Kabul: this marked the defeat of the Taliban and heralded another decade of warfare for Afghanistan. Some of these tanks came out of the last of Russia's former Cold War reserves. (*Via Author*)

Satellite imagery of Taliban armour knocked out by American air strikes in the hills outside Herat. In reality most of these tanks were already scrap. (*US DoD*)

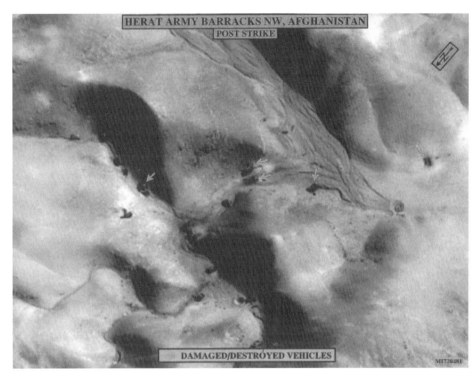

HERAT ARMY BARRACKS NW, AFGHANISTAN
POST STRIKE

DAMAGED/DESTROYED VEHICLES

MI720581

Another Soviet-era relic, the rusting remains of a BTR APC. (*US DoD*)

The Afghan Army is reborn with the assistance of its NATO allies. A refurbished T-62M main battle tank of the Afghan National Army in Kabul, photographed in April 2004. (*Davric*)

Two more T-62s of the Afghan National Army. No one can miss the irony that it is still equipped with Soviet-era weaponry. (*Davric*)

The Afghan National Army parading with an equally ancient Scud-B surface-to-surface missile. (*US DoD*)

An impressive array of Cold War tanks. Men of the Afghan National Army's 1st Armoured Battalion with their refurbished T-62s and T-62Ms in the spring of 2003. (*US DoD*)

Afghan National Army soldiers in Gayan district, Afghanistan during the first-ever democratic elections held in the country in October 2004. These elections did not bring peace or end the war with the Taliban. (*US DoD*)